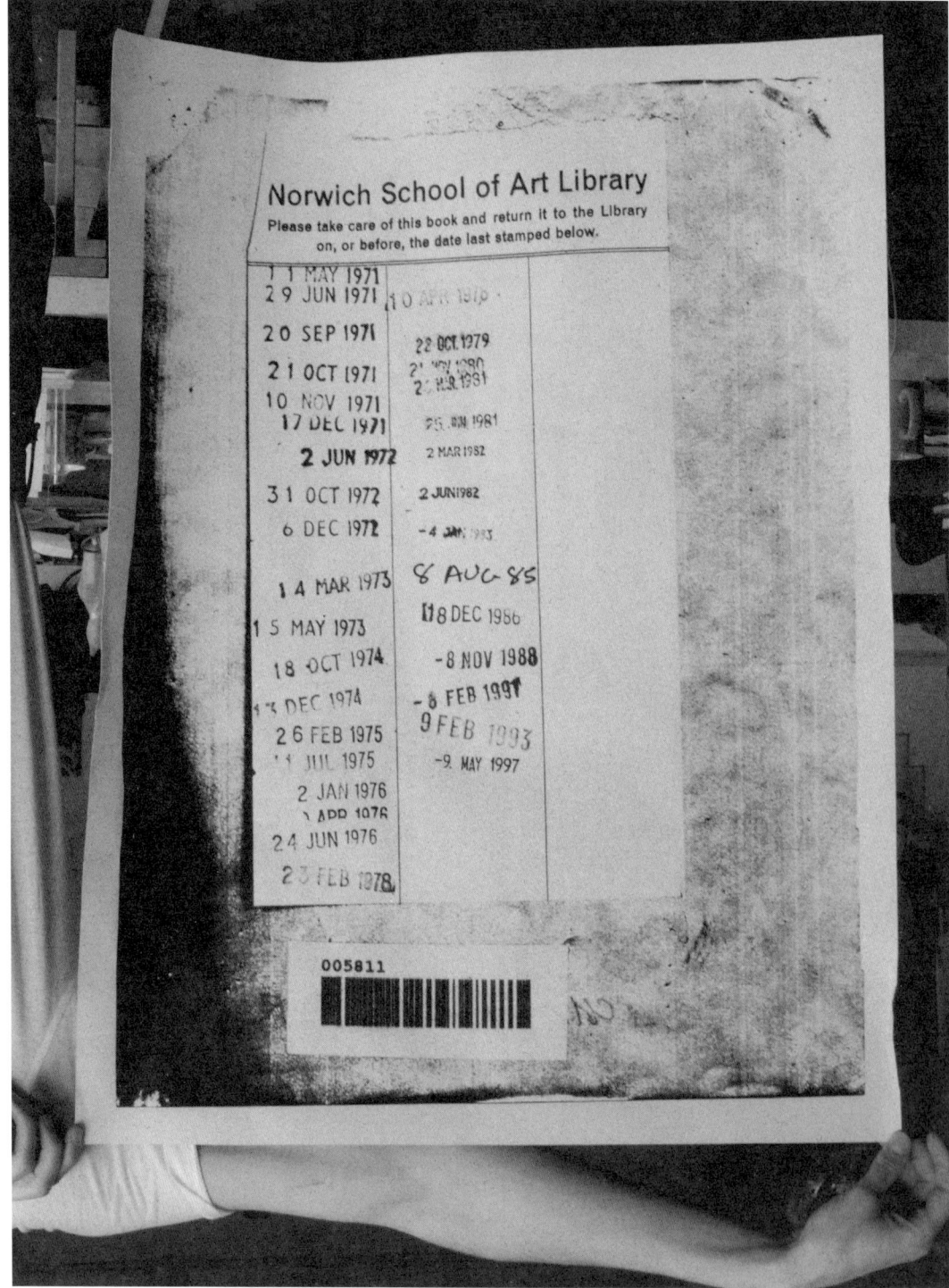

Luke Gottelier
*Norwich School of Art Library*
2007
Silkscreen on paper
80 x 62 cm
Poster commissioned to fund this publication.

Frontispiece on previous page:
Francis Upritchard
*Luke Gottelier, Brian Griffiths, Sam Basu and Francis Upritchard*
2004
29.7 x 21 cm
Portrait produced for the Essl Collection, Vienna.

*Bart Wells Institute*
First published in the UK by Dent-De-Leone 2009 — www.dentdeleone.co.nz

All rights reserved. No part of this book may be reprinted, reproduced or utilised in any form or by any electronic, mechanical or other means, now known or hereafter invented, including photocopying and recording, or in any information storage or retrieval system, without permission in writing from the publishers.

ISBN 978-0-9561885-2-6
A CIP catalogue record for this book is available from the British Library.

Edited by Luke Gottelier, Francis Upritchard, Sam Basu, Harry Pye and åbäke.
Written by Heather Galbraith, Sally O'Reilly, Martin Herbert, Brian Griffiths, Bruce Haines, David Thorpe, Mark Aerial Waller, Luke Gottelier, åbäke, Francis Upritchard, Sam Basu, Gianpaolo Cottino, Dan Fox and Harry Pye.

Designed by åbäke, London and printed by Die Keure, Bruges.
Photography: Francis Upritchard, Jet, Jim Flint, Antonia Horrocks, Goshka Macuga, Sam Basu, Mark Aerial Waller, Hari Kunzru, FXP Photography, Harry Pye, Leigh McCarthy, Stuart Cumberland, John Spiteri, Frank Hannon, Daria Martin, Eva Berendes, Nicholas Stewart, Jonnie Basset, Cedar Lewisohn, Milena Dragicevic, Gianpaolo Cottino, Florian Balze, Luke Gottelier, Scott Myles, Hayley Tompkins, Ulli Knall, åbäke and anyone else who slipped through the net.

Texts, images © the authors and the artists

Acknowledgments: Yana Peel, Candida Gertler and all at Outset, Jamie King, Lawrence O'Hana, Johnny Vivash, Leigh McCarthy, Jet, Jess Search, The Cock Rockers, David Panos, Kate MacGarry, Fabio Altamura, Susie Clark, Liz Murray, Hari Kunzru, Jake Miller, Vanessa Carlos, Katy Partridge, Siraj Izhar, Maureen Paley, Katie Guggenheim, Julia Hoelz, Luis Zavala, Mat Humphrey, Sarah Jones, Olivia Lory Kay, Kath Roper-Caldbeck, Norwegian Lady, Some Product, Pillow Fight, Mark Corcoran, The Annoying Cowboys, Adrian Teenbeat, Snakes, Ghost Club, Go Feral, Petcar, Art School Graduate, Donna Huddleston, Megan Jones, Suneil Basu, Peter McDonald, Alice Cowling, Keith Wilson, Kaavous Clayton, Jane Bhoyroo, Conor Donlon, Hannah Upritchard, Jarrod Rawlins and George Asciak

Cover and back cover: The Bart Wells Institute in 2002 and 2007
Endpapers: Bart Wells Institute main entrance; Bart Wells Institute publication proposals by Harry Pye

This book was published in a limited edition of 1,000 copies. The first 50 copies are complete sets of uncollated Bart Wells Institute Periodicals enclosed with a sheet of signed and numbered Bart Wells Institute letterhead.

Supported by:

# INTRODUCTION

I heard about the Bart Wells Institute in 2001 through artist friends – a new space was opening up in Hackney, run by artists. An invitation for the first show landed in our postbox titled *The Bart Wells Gang*, with an address I didn't recognise. The name sounded official, authoritative – an Institute no less. There was a logo, sketchily hand-drawn, flecked with coloured ink, signalling that this might be a different type of entity. And as to who the hell Bart Wells was, well at that stage, we were none the wiser.

Scouring the *A to Z*, I found Silesia Buildings, which despite the "Buildings" part was actually a slip of a road I had never noticed before, curling off the main drag of Mare Street. The first visit to the Institute was on a cold December night in 2001. Stumbling up a dark, uneven-surfaced road (I want to say it was made of cobblestones, but this may be a Dickensian memory trick), there wasn't much evidence of a throng. The ground floor of the stripped-out brick building with its precariously outward-leaning front was devoid of people. Ascending the narrow rickety staircase, the crowd on the middle floor had thickened to about six, but on reaching the top level the draw-cards were obvious – the bar and the open smoking fire.

*The Bart Wells Gang* included work by Sam Basu, Harry Pye, Mick Mee and the two founders of the space, Luke Gottelier and Francis Upritchard. It was to be the first of eight shows, each curated by a different artist over the next year and a half. Francis and Luke had come across the building – clogged with acres of pigeon shit, soggy clothes and cardboard. They and other artists set about emptying out the building and stripping it back to its bare bones and created a gallery space where they could make shows.

The interior spaces were gradually "improved" over time, edging one show at a time closer to a classic white space, but as the tongue-in-cheek, highfaluting name conveys, it was never an aspiration for the Bart Wells Institute to become over-professionalised or institutionalised. In addition to the exhibitions there was: a concurrent curated film programme, a music programme with live bands (which also served a parallel function as fundraisers for the ongoing programme) and an artist's residency. There was not a whiff of public money or private patronage at the Bart Wells Institute. The space was run through the efforts of the "directors" Francis Upritchard and Luke Gottelier and key collaborating artists such as Sam Basu and Brian Griffiths, and was financed by beer sales at openings which funded mailouts and building materials.

The name Bart Wells Institute was inspired by Mick Mee, an elderly urban cowboy who had a pine door stripping workshop nearby on Sylvester Road. The workshop was festooned with handmade cowboy sets and paraphernalia. Mick Mee called it *Cowboy Street* and everything inside was either made simply or found on the streets of Hackney. He would often turn up to work in full cowboy regalia. Mick Mee roved around Hackney on his tricycle with his mates and dog in tow raising money for St. Joseph's Hospice. Everyone who helped raise money for the Hospice was given a cowboy name and in exchange for lending some of his paraphernalia for the first exhibition, Mick Mee requested that Luke Gottelier spend a day fundraising. He was given the moniker "Lucky Luke – the ballroom swindler," which brings us back to the derivation of the name Bart Wells Institute. For a spell one of Mick Mee's fellow fundraisers had the pseudonym "Bart Wells" and the whole charitable troupe were known as "The Bart Wells Gang." But "Bart Wells" absconded to America and the name was abandoned. An elegant sign in Mick Mee's distinctive handwriting spelling out the legend "The Bart Wells Gang" was lying around in his workshop and was opportunistically co-opted for the title of the first exhibition and, with a subtle swapping of "institute" for "gang," became the name of the endeavour. Although Mick Mee would not have considered himself an artist, *Cowboy Street* exemplified the spirit of Bart Wells Institute: make it cheap, don't pay unless you have to, use what is at your fingertips and make it by hand. At the gallery a tiny bell hung from a long piece of ribbon descending from the second to the ground floor was the doorbell. It usually got rung off its perch, and had to be continually reattached. Hollering also sometimes worked.

The first couple of shows used all three floors. The second exhibition, *The Suitcase Show*, was an exchange with Los Angeles. The whole show was packed into a suitcase and flown to America. One

Francis Upritchard's studio at Bart Wells Institute

came back in the opposite direction comprising the show in London. The third show *The Necessary Enemy* was curated by Brian Griffiths. A sort of curatorial haunted house, the show included Simon Bill, David Thorpe and John Spiteri. Further shows included *Viva Pablo* curated by Harry Pye, which was based on the premise that Picasso hadn't died in 1973 and had been churning out masterpieces in Hackney ever since. Each artist exhibiting was asked to make a work for a year from 1973 to the present. Sam Basu organised the gothic monstrosity *Tombs of the Fantasy Undead* which included Goshka Macuga's haunting, playfully macabre installation *Salon*. The final show was David Thorpe's lo-fi epic *The Fragile Underground* which questioned the notion of an artistic underground and included the work of Scott Myles, Eva Berendes, Hayley Tompkins and Daria Martin.

Artist-run initiatives and not-for-profit project spaces have been vital components of art communities since the middle of the twentieth century with London furnishing a particularly dense concentration from the late 1980s through to now. These more recent endeavours had significant precursors and an all-too-brief skim across early contributors alights upon: the Artists' Placement Group formed in 1966 with key contributors artists John Latham and Barbara Steveni; the Centre of Advanced Creative Study founded in 1964 by artist David Medalla; SPACE Studios and AIR (Artists' Information Registry) which were formed in the late 1960s, through to the seminal Matt's Gallery founded by Robin Klassnik, which came into being alongside ACME Studios in 1979.

To contextualize the Bart Wells Institute it is useful to look at the kinds of projects active in

London in the ten years prior to and concurrent with its own brief but intense duration (2001–03). Artist-run initiatives have always been very varied, and this decade of activity in London was no different. Sometimes energies were channeled to a fixed gallery or project space (such as The Tannery, Beaconsfield, Independent Art Space). Often, but not always, these spaces were associated with a studio complex, such as Adam Gallery, Cubitt, Curtain Road Arts, Gasworks, Milch and 30 Underwood Street. Equally they could take the form of artist networks or groups (Bank), itinerant projects mounted in non-gallery sites (Space Explorations, Rear Window) and archives or publishing projects (Untitled, Implicasphere). Some ventures have lasted a very long time, becoming more stable in their infrastructure and acquiring regular public funding, while others have lasted as long as the momentum and energy of their instigators/collaborators.

By the time Bart Wells Institute came into being, the scene was radically different from that of the 1960s and 1970s, even from the heady mid to late Nineties with the legacy of exhibitions such as *Freeze*, *Modern Medicine*, *Gambler* and *Market*. The primary shift was the rising dominance of the art market, combined with a sometimes sluggish public gallery sector. While more cash was exchanging hands in certain circles, the trickledown was yet to hit emerging practitioners and there was still a great drive to be self-determined, to make projects that served the participating artists and their network of peers. The social economy of spaces such as the Bart Wells Institute should not be underrated.

Word of mouth, beginning with artists' networks, had spread rapidly and the Bart Wells Institute soon became known as a place you could see new work by artists "on the ascent." The space was included in mainstream listings, received national and international reviews and editorial. At the same time the artists running the space started to get busier with their own practices, and the significant energy required to run a programme in a crumbling building on sweet-bugger-all needed to be channelled into their own work. By the beginning of 2003, it was time for Bart Wells Institute to close its doors. This was just as the somewhat incongruous sight of well-healed collectors in flash private cars – sometimes complete with drivers – and institutional curators or directors alighting from black cabs was becoming regular.

When it ended, a real momentum of programming had developed, as had a tangible buzz about the space. But it was an unspoken aim between the directors and their collaborators to enjoy the Institute's temporal nature and not to be afraid to call it quits, or explore other possible incarnations of the entity. Indeed after the Institute was vacated three international exhibitions took place in Vienna, Berlin and Wellington.

Around this time Hackney was becoming sought after real estate for swanky warehouse developments. The forward-leaning fascia of 3 Silesia Buildings was demolished along with the rest of the building to make way for new construction. However, the extended crew of artists, writers, curators, musicians and filmmakers involved struck friendships and professional relationships which have long outlasted the lifespan of the precarious bricks and mortar of the Bart Wells Institute.

— Heather Galbraith

# BART WELLS INSTITUTE

# 01. THE NAME

cf. p. v

## DEFINITION OF AN ARTIST-RUN SPACE

The traditional image of an artist-run space generally involves anarchic happenings, maverick exhibitions and left-of-field remits. Think of the Young Unknowns gallery in The Cut, in Waterloo during the 1980s, where work was shown anonymously in a two fingered gesture to the burgeoning celebrity-studded art scene of the time. And this was also the gallery that was taken to court for exhibiting the infamous foetus earrings that offended Mary Whitehouse and cronies. Surely this is the sort of scandalous repute we desire, with all involved running full tilt at conventions and chucking around taboos like confetti?

But the artist-run space is not so radical these days, it seems. Being an artist can now be so professionalised that it is hard to tell the difference between a gallery run by someone who does and someone who doesn't make work themselves. Since entrepreneurial ventures such as the *Freeze* exhibition that launched the whole tiring notion of the yBas, the profile, remit and methodology of such initiatives has changed from bloodyminded contrariness to stolid self-determination. Because why would an artist want to cut off or provoke peers or collectors who represent a means of support, whether moral or financial? And if the institutional critique of the 1970s taught us anything it is that a position within the host institution is the best position from which to illuminate its machinations or manipulate it to one's own ends.

Bart Wells Institute is one in a long list of transitory artist-run spaces that have contributed to London's reputation as a nodal point for the art world, and the Institute sits right on the cusp between the old guard and the new savvy. The founders and their associates are not quite of the überprofessional generation that can hustle three international supercurators before breakfast; but then neither are they particularly

# BART WELLS INSTITUTE

## 02. IDENTITY GUIDELINES

    a.  Use the cheapest possible means
    b.  Use what is easily available
    c.  Make it look easy
    d.  If it's wonky, accept it
    e.  Turn the problem into an asset
    f.  Style is a fallacy
    g.  Everybody is an expert

"smash the system" types either. Quite simply, setting up their own space allowed this group of artists to do the things they wanted in the way they wished. Like the collective Bank before them they could over-thematise a show until the aesthetic of its installation nearly obliterated the work by other artists in it, as in Goshka Macuga's system of industrial chains from which she hung paintings, which lent *Tombs of the Fantasy Undead* a musclebound edge. And as with City Racing, the artist-run space in Vauxhall that operated throughout the 1990s, those involved could unabashedly nurture a clique by inviting their mates, and mates of mates, to exhibit or contribute (present author included) – a nepotistic no-no in public art institutions and commercial galleries.

The Bart Wells building itself would also have given an institutional health and safety officer a conniption: it was crumbling, cracked and gappy almost to the point of ruin. It was damp, cold and bloody dangerous, impossible to insure and a challenge to a pair of white slacks. But, as one of the last old school squats, it was free. Now that the law has changed to hand rights firmly over to property owners and a number of companies have begun to install temporary residents to keep uninvited squatters out, the commercial property sector closes down a lot of operations before they've even begun.

At times the inevitable mend-and-make-do approach of the unfunded project space elicits some charming solutions – a show brought over from Los Angeles in a suitcase made for a pleasing smuggling back story – at others it was simply a drag. Someone had to stay in the building at all times, producing something of siege mentality among the artists, curators and invigilators. Perhaps it was this "us against them" atmosphere that eventually wears out an outfit like Bart Wells. Or maybe it was the way that press coverage, at first buoyant, tailed off as the lack of a marketing department meant that public interest inevitably

h. Everything is in the mistake
i. Don't deliberate
j. Cultivate imperfection
k. Vulgarity is the highest form of art
l. Have fun

moved on to the next novelty. Or perhaps the artists wondered why on earth they were struggling to curate a space when they ultimately wanted to make their own work. Why double up your job description when so many art colleges are training up and shipping out curators by the baker's dozen?

That most artist-run spaces eventually disappear, whether through being disbanded, or installing a director and converting into a business or institution, never comes as a great surprise. There are a few exceptions, such as Transmission Gallery in Glasgow, which has been self-governing for nearly two decades, but just as the supposed democratic openness of the world wide web has been colonised by new hierarchies, the artist-run space soon gives way to pressure to either crystallise into some sort of bureaucratic structure or dissolve altogether. It seems that the reason societies are underpinned by regulatory bodies, chains of command and limiting boundaries is that doing everything for yourself, inventing methodologies from scratch and learning the limits of what is workable each time is just too enervating. It remains vital, though, that these short flashes of recalcitrant self-determination continue to ignite, as the light they throw on innate power structures is illuminating indeed.

— Sally O'Reilly

# BART WELLS INSTITUTE

# 03. THE ARTISTS

Shahin Afrassiabi [b2]
Phillip Allen [f]
Artlab
  (Cullinan Richards) [b2 d]
Florian Balze [h]
Sam Basu [a g]
Diann Bauer [b2]
Eva Berendes [h]
Gordon Beswick [e]
Simon Bill [c]
Amy Blount [b1]
Jeff Brady [b1]
Matt Bryans [d]
Matt Calderwood [e]
Clare Ceprynski [b2]
Billy Childish [e f]
Lee Clarke [b1]
Henry Coleman [d]
Dan Connor [e]
Chris Coombes [e]
Gianpaolo Cottino [f]
Elidh Crumlish [e]
Stuart Cumberland [e]
Cuong Sam [e]
Jeremy Deadman [c]
Zeyad Dejani [b2]
Milena Dragicevic [d]
Sean Duffy [b1]
Robin Forster
  & James Barrett [b2]
Sharan Gillespie [b1]
Luke Gottelier [a b2 e f]
Kevin Francis Gray [b2 d]
Brian Griffiths [c]
Johnny Gunshenan [b2 d]
Liz Haarala [e]
Sarah Dawn Hampton [b1]

Frank Hannon [b2 d]
Peter Harris [e]
Emma Holmes [g]
Graham Hudson
  & Dave Hoyland [b2]
Mat Humphrey [e]
Runa Islam [b2]
Mark Jackson [e]
Jasper Joffe [e]
Ulli Knall [h]
Deb Lacusta [b1]
Debbie Lawson [c]
Cedar Lewisohn [g]
David Lock [b2]
Keila Lopez [b1]
Colin Lowe
  & Roddy Thomson [f]
Geoff Lucas [e]
Peter Lynch [c]
Leigh McCarthy [b2]
Faris McReynolds [b1]
Goshka Macuga [g]
Daria Martin [h]
Mick Mee [a]
Karen Morden
  & Paul Hamilton [e]
John Moseley [e]
Andrew Mottershead [e]
Paul Munn [e]
Scott Myles [h]
David Noonan [d]
Humphrey Ocean [e]
Chris Owen [e]
Mark Pearson [c]
Terri Phillips [b1]
Olivia Plender [e]
Stuart Purdy [d]

Harry Pye [a e]
The Pye Family [e]
Vincent Ramos [b1]
Jacob Rhodes [b1]
Kes Richardson [e]
Mark Roeder [b1]
Ed Scotland [e]
Veronica Seifert
  & Cordelia Underhill [e]
Adrian R. Shaw [e]
Adam Shepherd [e]
Anna Shepherd
  & Janet Hamilton-Gill [e]
Bob and Roberta Smith [b2]
Rowland Smith [e]
Soo Kim [b1]
John Spiteri [c]
Nicholas Stewart [c]
Tommy Støckel [h]
Therese Stowell [b2]
David Thorpe [c]
Anik Todd [e]
Hayley Tompkins [h]
Francis Upritchard [a e f]
Tracy Urabe [b1]
Johnny de Veras [e]
Jessica Voorsanger [b2]
Edward Ward [e]
Caroline Warde [g]
Richard Wathen [e]
Benjamin Weissman [b1]
Kit Wise [e]
Christine Wolfe [b2]
Simon Woolham [d]
Yunhee Min [b1]

# BART WELLS INSTITUTE

# 04. TIMELINE

| | | | |
|---|---|---|---|
| a  | 15 December 2001 – 26 January 2002 | THE BART WELLS GANG | p. 01 |
| b1 | 16 February 2002 – 23 March 2002 | THE SUITCASE SHOW, London | p. 17 |
| b2 | 8 February 2002 – 23 February 2002 | THE SUITCASE SHOW, Los Angeles | |
| c  | 19 April 2002 – 2 June 2002 | THE NECESSARY ENEMY | p. 33 |
| d  | 22 June 2002 – 21 July 2002 | MAY IT RETURN IN SPADES | p. 49 |
| e  | 3 August 2002 – 8 September 2002 | VIVA PABLO | p. 65 |
| f  | 21 September 2002 – 3 November 2002 | ANOTHER SHITTY DAY IN PARADISE | p. 81 |
| g  | 16 November 2002 – 22 December 2002 | TOMBS OF THE FANTASY UNDEAD | p. 97 |
| h  | 1 February 2003 – 9 March 2003 | THE FRAGILE UNDERGROUND | p. 113 |

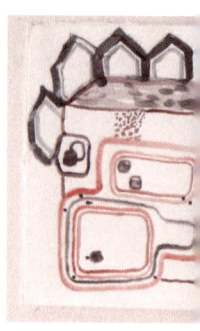
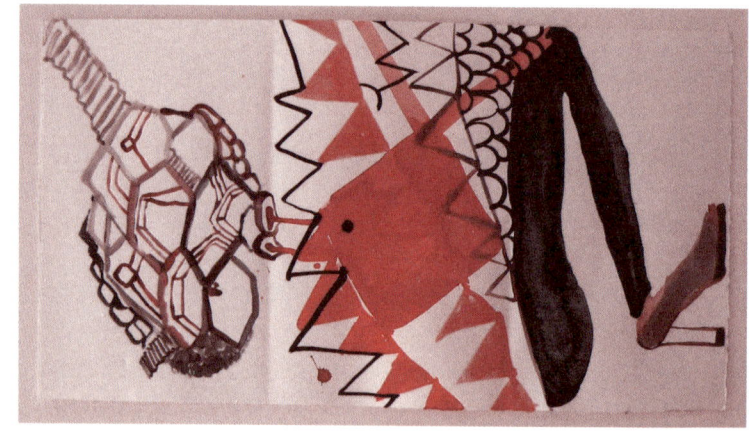
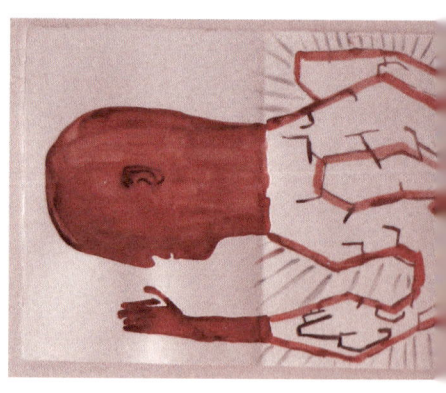

BART WELLS INSTITUTE

05. THE REMUNERATION OF THE WRITERS

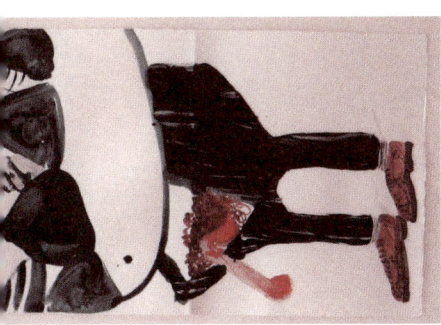

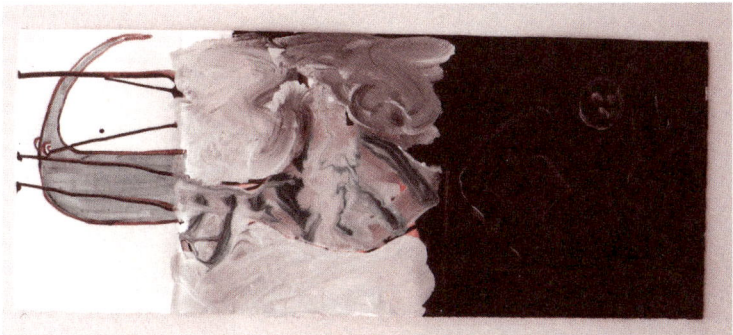

Exquisite corpses by Francis Upritchard, Sam Basu and Luke Gottelier

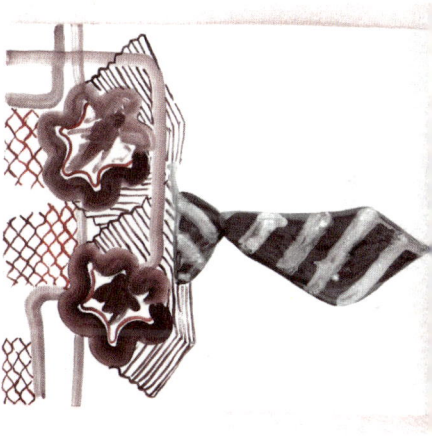

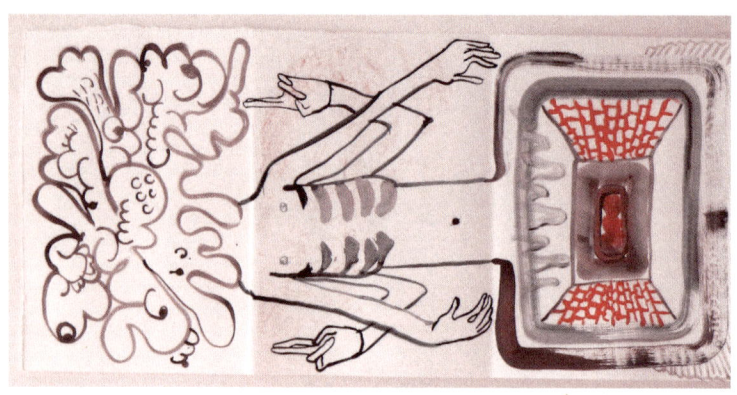

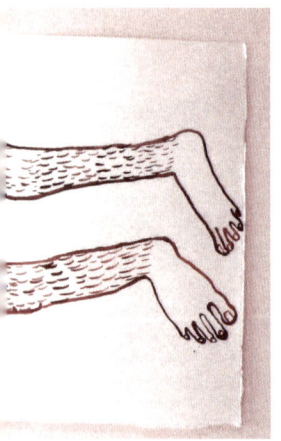

Sam Basu
*Basuhaus Way of Discipline*
2007
Silkscreen on found poster
80 x 56.5 cm
Poster commissioned to fund this publication.

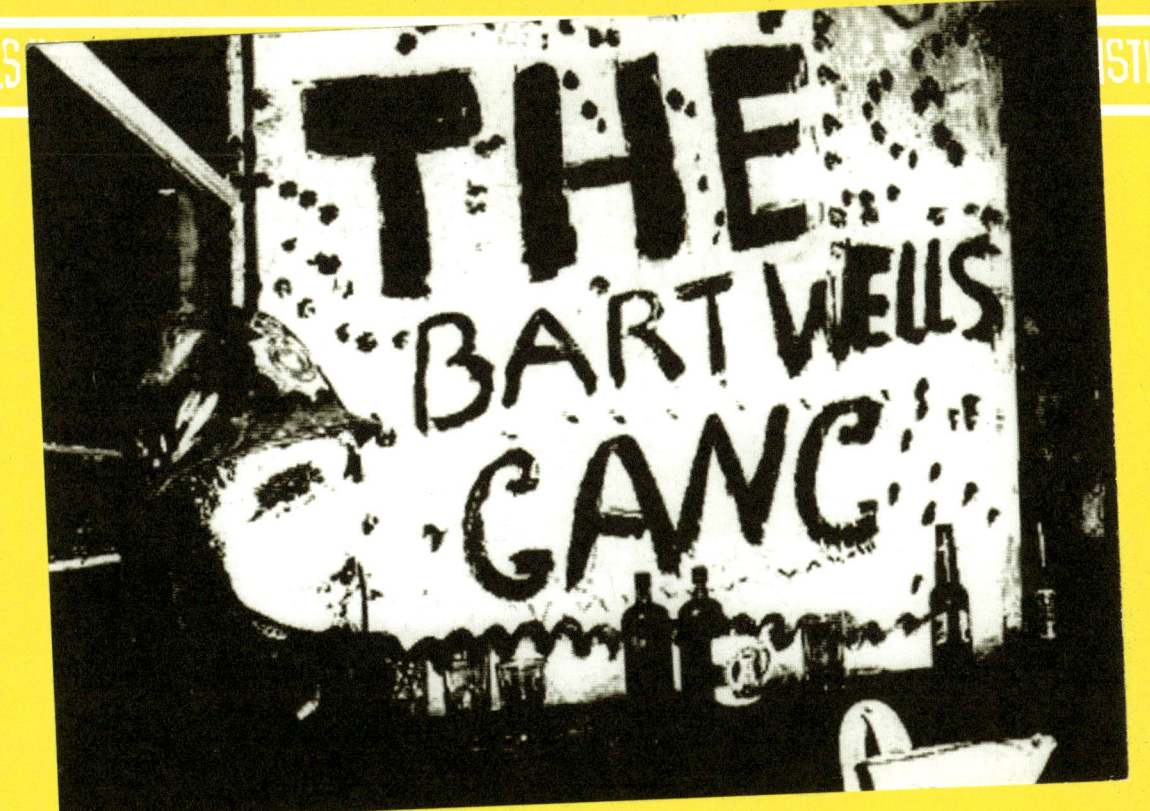

# PERIODICAL

NUMBER 1

WINTER 2001

£1

3 Silesia Buildings, London E8

# The Bart Wells Gang

Sam Basu
Francis Upritchard
Harry Pye
Mick Mee
Luke Gottelier

**Opening Friday 14th December 6-8pm**
Saturday 15th December 2001 - Saturday 26th January 2002

Open Saturdays 12-6pm   Exhibition closed Saturday 29th December
3 Silesia Buildings, off London Lane, London E8

Luke Gottelier
*The Bon Bonny*
2001
Oil and acrylic on canvas
122 x 102 cm

# THE BART WELLS GANG EXHIBITION

Sam Basu will be exhibiting two films; PSYKICK BOXER, made in collaboration with Gower Ramsey and DOG TYPE MAGIC. He will also be exhibiting sculptures.

Mick Mee, formerly of The Bart Wells Gang, and currently of The Mick Mee Gang, is 75 and has never been to art college. There will be a presentation of his objects from COWBOY STREET, a.k.a The Sundown Saloon

Luke Gottelier will be exhibiting five new paintings including "Self-Portrait as Luther Being Played by The Devil as a Pair of Bagpipes". Gottelier studied Fine Art at Norwich School of Art 2000-2001

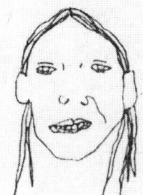

Francis Upritchard studied Fine Art at Ilam School of Art, Christchurch, New Zealand. She will be exhibiting a group of works "The Curse of the Mummy"

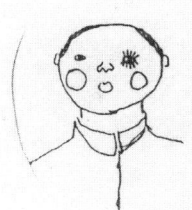

Harry Pye and his friends will be exhibiting his nominations for the Turner Prize 2002. Crossing a range of contemporary media this show will include a lifesize sculpture of Harry Pye. Harry Pye founded "Harry Pye's Frank Magazine" in 1995 and recently published "Moving Target III" and "The A to B of Culture"

Live at opening
SNAKES
plus
ADRIAN SHAW AND
THE SMITHS GARRET BAND

Curated by Francis Upritchard

The Bart Wells Gang Exhibition: 3 Silesia Buildings, London E8   020 7739 7228
Opening Friday 14th December 6-9pm. Sat 15th December 2001 - Saturday 26th January 2002.
Open Saturdays 12-6pm or by appointment.

# Turner Prize 2002

3 Silesia Buildings, off London Lane E8
Open on Saturdays from 12 – 6pm.
15th December 01 to 26th of January 02
(Closed on Sat 29th December)

## Introduction
By John Moseley

For 17 happy years now, the Turner Prize exhibition has been confounding, delighting and amazing visitors to its berth in the sumptuous surroundings of the Tate Britain Galleries. Always outrageous, compelling, never boring, the Turner Prize gives a normally art-starved public the opportunity to view the work of thrilling, cutting-edge artists to whom 'they' might normally never have been exposed. The statistics are testament alone. Each year an average of 75,000 visitors throng the exhibition of the nominees' work and emerge challenged, dismayed, upset, delighted and so on. What we can say for certain is that no one ever comes away feeling let down, disillusioned or, of course, bored. But what exactly is The Turner Prize? For the uninitiated, a summary: each year, four artists under fifty are given the chance to compete for the title of 'Best Artist'.

This year, the shortlisted artists are Harry Pye, Harry Pye, Harry Pye and Harry Pye. I don't believe it is putting the cart before the horse to say that the winner will almost certainly be Harry Pye, a young artist whose work has been closer than anyone to the aims of the Turner Prize throughout his career. But let us hold off on such speculation for the moment at least and allow ourselves the heart-pounding excitement of simply not knowing right up until the moment when the visiting dignitary ascends the podium and announces, 'Ladies and gentlemen, it gives me great pleasure to announce that this year's best artist is…'

## Sponsor's Forward

"Throughout its history, the Turner Prize has gone out of its way to court controversy. To make matters worse, year after year we've seen examples of political correctness gone mad. Previous judges of the Turner Prize for example, have taken anti-racism to the ludicrous extreme of actually not being racist. However, in light of Tate Britain recent decision to adopt a common sense "No Irish, No Blacks, No Dogs" policy, The Conservative Party are delighted to be associated with the Turner Prize. At last! Four nominees – all normal men and all properly British. Don't let the curry stained, drug taking perverts have their day!"
Iain Duncan Smith, leader of the Conservative Party.

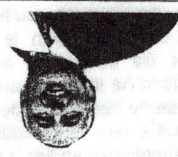

## Previous winners of the Turner Prize

1984: Midge Ure
1985: The cast of Grange Hill
1986: Zippy & George
1987: Patsy Kensit
1988: Your Dad
1989: Your Mum
1990: *Prize suspended*
1991: Snoop Doggy Dog
1992: Grenville Davey
1993: Rachel Whiteread & The KLF
1994: Alex James from Blur
1996: Michael Barrymoore
1997: Gillian Wearing
1998: Lenny Henry
1999: Craig David
2000: Gary Glitter
2001: Jonathan King

## The shortlisted artists are:

**Harry Pye,** for his contribution to 'Record Collection' at the VTO Gallery in Bethnal Green last April and for being the reality of ideals, the verity of joy and the proof of goodness.

**Harry Pye,** for his video collaboration with Gordon Beswick ("Harry Pye's Love Story") screened at Rosemary School in Farringdon as part of "Blowing Up" last August and for being the power of gentleness, beauty's acknowledgement and vanity's excuse.

**Harry Pye,** for not only, his other video collaboration with Gordon Beswick (an all-star re-make of the 'Goodbyee' theme tune) screened at "Why Bother? The 4th meeting of the Peter Cook Appreciation Society" at The Bath House in Soho last November. But also, for being the promise of truth, the melody of life and the caress of romance.

**Harry Pye,** for his editorship of "The A to B of Culture" magazine (made in collaboration with Daniel Connor, Paul Hamilton, Adrian Shaw & Ed Ward) last October and also for being your belief in heaven, the sanctuary of your soul and the dream of desire.

Harry Pye can be contacted via:
harry_pye@hotmail.com and also
www.frankmagazine.co.uk

# Harry Pye

**1973**: Born in Lewisham
**1984 – 91**: Crown Woods Comprehensive & 6th Form College.

The message of "Three Harry Pyes sitting at a table with a hat on it" could well be as straightforward as, Give Peace A Chance. During the duration of previous wars that took place in his lifetime (Vietnam, The Falklands, The Gulf etc) Pye always kept a dignified silence. What is it about Bush 'n' Blaire's current tiff with so-called terrorist bin Laden that makes Pye want to speak out? As somebody clever once observed, "Inept, law, Three Jones's The slave nothing to do with demanding justice and ends by losing be hurts. a crown." Why is it that the slave (or she) must dominate in alphabet! slave just stop after he justice? Why does the slave away and insistent on a change
In "Three Harry Pye's sitting at a table with a hat on it" we see the artist in 3 stages. 1) Pretending to ignore the Fez. 2) Smiling as the Fez falls into his grasp. 3) Rejecting the Fez (or "the Crown") and looking slightly annoyed. Is the artist commenting on a certain turbaned Ruffian whose recently got too big for his sandals? Or, is he saying something outrageous about New Labour? It would probably be easier to say what he *isn't* saying than what he is.
Whatever he's saying he's saying it in his own special way, just like that.

# Harry Pye

**1991-92**: Camberwell School of Art
**1992-95**: Winchester School of Art

Whether it's a kiss in the dark or a walk in the park, everybody likes THINGS. To be boring for a moment, the only 'thing' in the material world that an artist inhabits is his or her own body. We exist within a particular perception of time frame and blah blah blah, and yet zzzzzzzzzzzzzz. The question of, 'How oh how oh how do you make an object that is obviously 3 dimensional, free-standing in a place that actually conveys an, if you like, void, a volume that's upon per-mache in the inhabits) and then decide to degree of success is the very same degree to which that paradox I mentioned earlier is resolved.

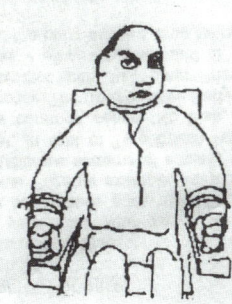

# Harry Pye

**1995**: Employed part-time as a projectionist at The Royal Astronomical Society and as a doorman at Lewisham Theatre.

Elizabeth Kubler-Ross, once wrote: "Every individual human being born on this earth has the capacity to become a unique and special person, unlike any who has ever existed before or will ever exist again. But to the extent that we become captives of culturally defined role expectations and behaviours – stereotypes, not ourselves – we block our capacity for self actualization."
Over the years Harry Pye has met a few unique and special people, mostly at private views. In "Harry Pye's Thank You List" the artist Harry Pye is listing the people he wants to say Thank You to. Is that so hard to understand?

> Damien, you were my bombers, my dexys, my high – thanks.
> David at Zwemmers – You run the best gallery in the whole damn world, man. Don't go changing.
> Jan and everybody at Stedelijk Van Abbemuseum – cheers!
> Jay Jopling, Jay, now you're all over your song is so tame, you fed, you bred me, I'll remember your name.
> John Gibbons, thank you for having a clue.
> Martin Creed – the first great man I ever met.
> Michael Craig-Martin, thanks Mike, sorry for taking you for granted.
> Pete Davies, you've been an inspiration.
> Thanks to Sarah and Martin and everyone at 'Time Out' who believe in me and dig my art and can see my heart.
> Tracey, I know I said some bad things about you and I know I hurt you but the fact you still want to be my friend means loads to me, really, it does.
> Wolfgang, if a man can love another man, I love you.

# Harry Pye

**1996 – Present**: Sales Assistant in bookshop at Tate Britain

"Rejection is one thing" the pop star Morrissey once sang, "But rejection from a fool is cruel". "Harry Pye's Love Story" is a film that deals with rejection but is the artist guilty of foolishness or cruelty? Let's look at the evidence.
Throughout last year Harry kept a video diary as he embarked upon, what would prove to be a series of dangerous liaisons with half a dozen young women. Despite explaining to them from the off that his commitments to his job as a sales assistant and his loyalty to Tate Britain were his number one priority, things became problematic. He was happy to see them for the 9 and a half week period between major Tate shows (such as 'Intelligence' and 'William Blake') but felt adamant that continuing their relationship once a new exhibition had begun would be unfair on them and that they deserved better.
Why did these attractive, intelligent young women, all full of hope and self-esteem (and seemingly out of Pye's league) believe that they would be the one who would change him? Why do we hurt the ones we love? What is love? And is video art any good?

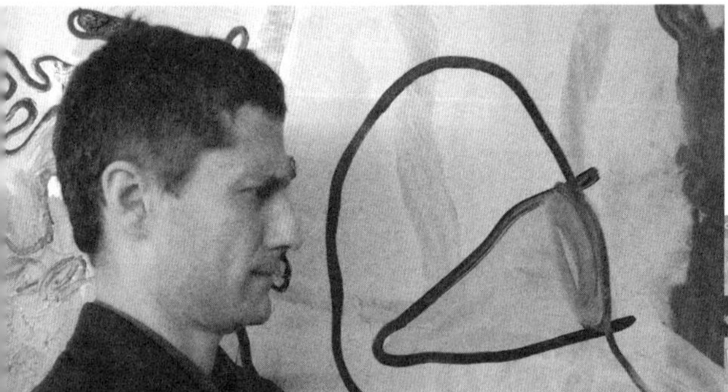

6

Anticlockwise from top left:

Photo of Harry Pye by Jonnie Basset made for
*Harry Pye's Turner Prize 2002*

Luke Gottelier in front of *The Bon Bonny*

Johnny de Veras with his painting made for
*Harry Pye's Turner Prize 2002*

Sam Basu with *Emerald Gateway*

Edward Ward presents us with his
Harry Pye drawings

Sculpture of Harry Pye made by Mat Humphrey
for *Harry Pye's Turner Prize 2002*

Previous double spread:
Francis Upritchard
*Save Yourself*
2001
Mixed media
99 x 34 cm
Courtesy Kate MacGarry,
London

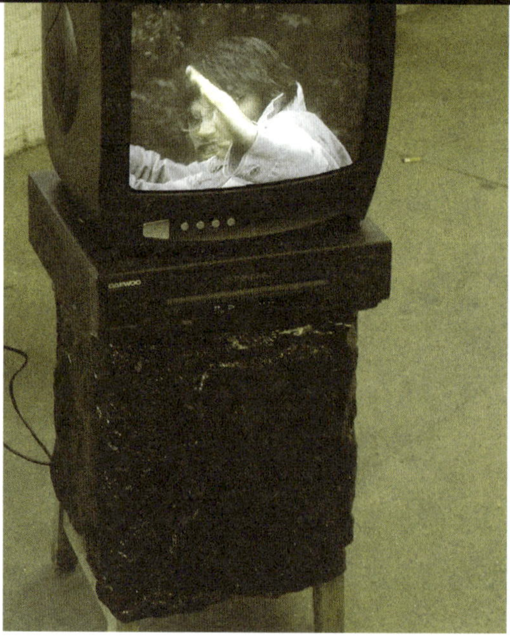

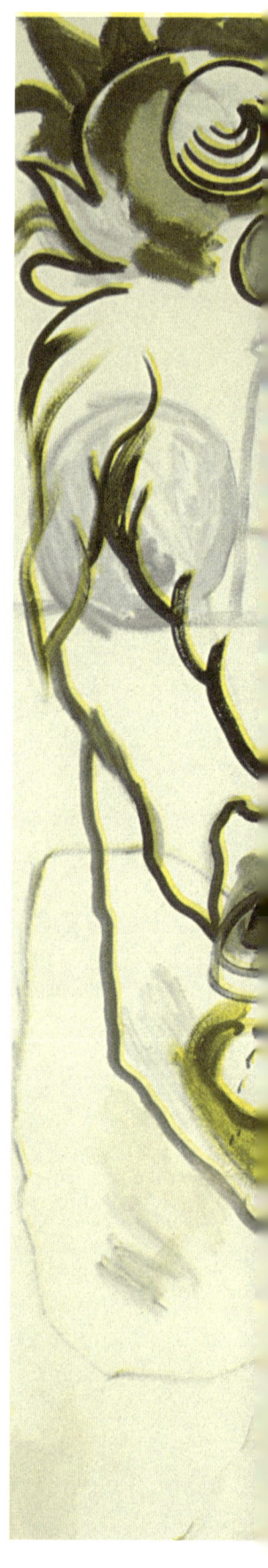

Sam Basu
*Psykick Boxer*
2001
Mini DVD video

Luke Gottelier
*Self-Portrait as Luther Being Played by The Devil as a Pair of Bagpipes*
2001
Oil and acrylic on canvas
122 x 107 cm

Sam Basu
Installation view
and stills from *Dog Type Magic*
2000
Super 8mm transferred to video

Mick Mee
Borrowed objects from *Cowboy Street*

The Mick Mee Gang
fundraising for St. Joseph's Hospice

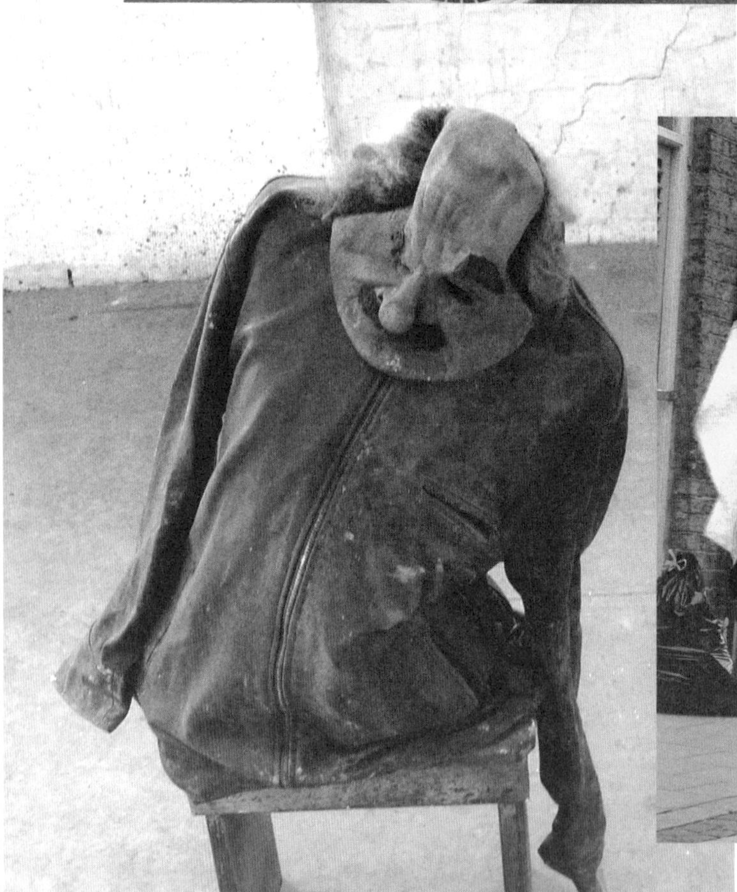

Luke Gottelier
*Eggy Head Bread*
2001
Oil and acrylic on canvas
122 x 102 cm

**BART WELLS INSTITUTE**  BART WELLS INSTITUTE  BART WELLS INSTITUTE

Single Copies
(incl. postage) £1
Annual Subscription
(6 issues, incl. postage) £5

---

I enclose £5 for 1 year's subscription to:

**BART WELLS INSTITUTE**

Name _____
Address _____
_____

Post to 3 Silesia Buildings, London E8

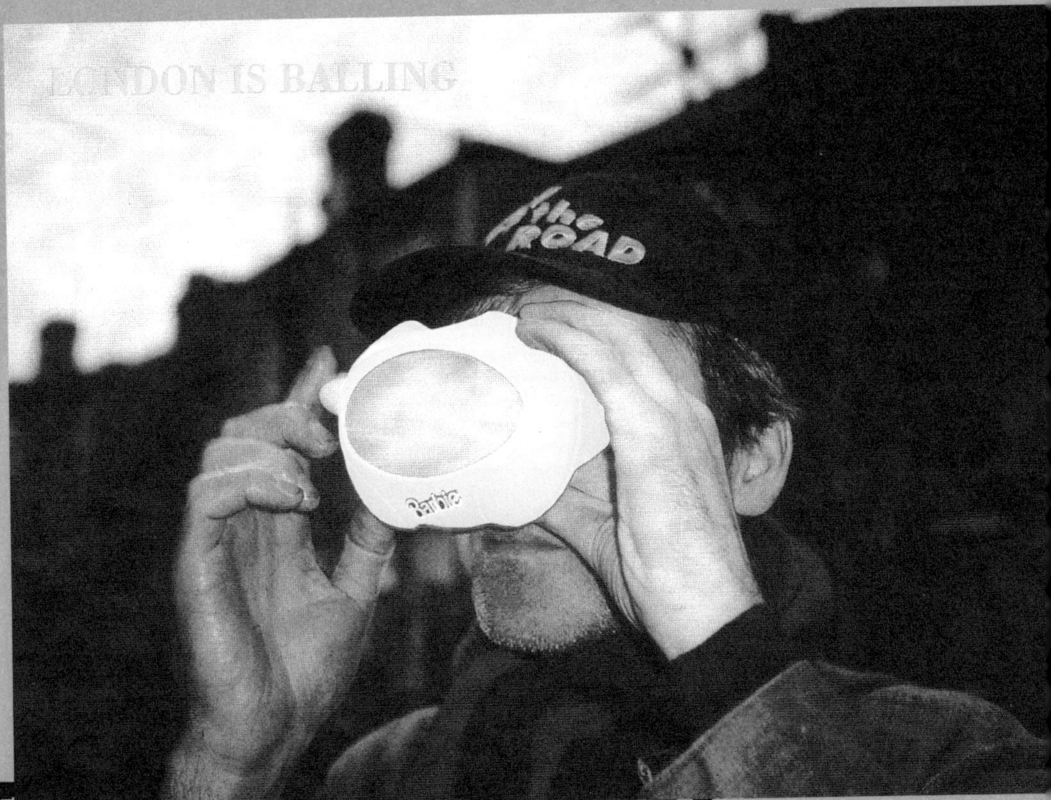
LONDON IS BALLING
the ROAD

# PERIODICAL #2.

BART WELLS INSTIT

2002.

1
5
0
$

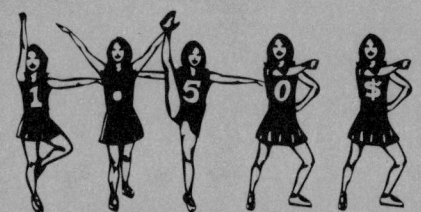

£1.00

# LONDON IS BALLING

PRIVATE VIEW 16 FEBRUARY
7PM - 10PM

16 FEBRUARY - 23 MARCH
OPEN SATURDAYS 12 - 6
OR BY APPOINTMENT

| | |
|---|---|
| AMY BLOUNT | FARIS MCREYNOLDS |
| JEFF BRADY | YUNHEE MIN |
| LEE CLARKE | TERRI PHILLIPS |
| SEAN DUFFY | VINCENT RAMOS |
| SHARAN GILLESPIE | JACOB RHODES |
| SARAH DAWN HAMPTON | MARK ROEDER |
| SOO KIM | TRACY UBARE |
| DURI ACOSTA | BENJAMIN WEISSMAN |
| KEILA LOPEZ | CURATED BY JACOB RHODES |

THE BARLWELLS INSTITUTE, 5 HUSTA BUILDINGS, OFF LONDON LANE, E8
TUBE: BETHNAL GREEN, THEN BUS D6, 106 OR 253
CONTACT: 0796 739 5838 OR INFO@SUITCASESHOW.COM OR WWW.SUITCASESHOW.COM

# THE SUITCASE SHOW

# BART WELLS INSTITUTE

3 Silesia Buildings, London E8

PRESS RELEASE FOR *THE SUITCASE SHOW*

The up and coming artcool of L.A. hits London on the 16th of February as "The Suitcase Show" makes its U.K. connection with "London is Balling" at the Bart Wells Institute. This show represents one side of a curated project by Leigh McCarthy and Jacob Rhodes, as EAST End meets WEST Coast; it should be a movie! The story goes like this; in early 2002, an exchange of unique contemporary baggage took place somewhere between Heathrow and LAX, the details of which remain secret. Each curator's mission; to exhibit the hand-picked artworks of the other's selection. Which incidentally had to fit into a "no excess charge" suitcase, packed with L.A. artists including Sean Duffy, Soo Kim, and Benjamin Weissman. There will also be a closing party with presentations from ArtLab, Graham Hudson and Dave Hoyland, and Leigh McCarthy. That evening Frank Hannon, Seb Patane, Bob and Roberta Smith, and Gavin Turk will be spinning the night away.

Rhodes' suitcase is open for all from February 16th – March 23rd 2002.

Private View Saturday 16th February 2002 7–10pm.

| *LONDON IS BALLING* ARTISTS | *ACROSS THE POND* ARTISTS |
|---|---|
| Amy Blount | Diann Bauer |
| Jeff Brady | Clare Ceprynski |
| Lee Clarke | David Lock |
| Sean Duffy | Robin Forster & James Barrett |
| Sharan Gillespie | Leigh McCarthy |
| Sarah Dawn Hampton | Therese Stowell |
| Soo Kim | Smalltown (Frank Hannon) |
| Deb Lacusta | Kevin Francis Gray & Luke Gottelier |
| Keila Lopez | Johnny Gunshenan |
| Faris McReynolds | ArtLab: Charlotte Cullinan and Jeanine Richards |
| Yunhee Min | Jessica Voorsanger |
| Terri Phillips | Bob and Roberta Smith |
| Vincent Ramos | Christine Wolfe |
| Jacob Rhodes | Runa Islam |
| Mark Roeder | Zeyad Dejani |
| Tracy Urabe | Graham Hudson & Dave Hoyland |
| Benjamin Weissman | Shahin Afrassiabi |

Curated by Jacob Rhodes

Curated by Leigh McCarthy

Private view Friday February 8th 2002 7–10pm.

Open February 8th – 23rd 2002
The Practice Space
5443 W. Pico
Los Angeles
USA

Open Saturdays 11–6pm or by appointment.

The next exhibition at the Bart Wells Institute will be *The Necessary Enemy* curated by Brian Griffiths.

For further information about *The Suitcase Show* telephone 07967 495 838. Email info@suitcaseshow.com.
Open Saturdays and Sundays 12-6pm.

The installation of *The Suitcase Show*

Artlab (Cullinan Richards)
*Pistol Range*
2002
Chinese pistols, leads, sculpture, rubbish
Variable dimensions

Terri Phillips
*Untitled*
2002
Sculpey
5 x 10 x 10 cm

*London is Balling* installation view with work by Mark Roeder, Vincent Ramos, Keila Lopez, Jacob Rhodes and Deb Lacusta

Kiela Lopez
*Boy Scout 22 (I Emo You!)*
2001
Silkscreen, coloured pencil and sticker on canvas
28 x 43 cm

Amy Blount
*Four Minute Lullaby*
2002
Acrylic and colour photocopies
28 x 20 x 18 cm

Next double spread:
Leigh McCarthy
*Heading Across the Pond*
2002
Photograph
10 x 15 cm

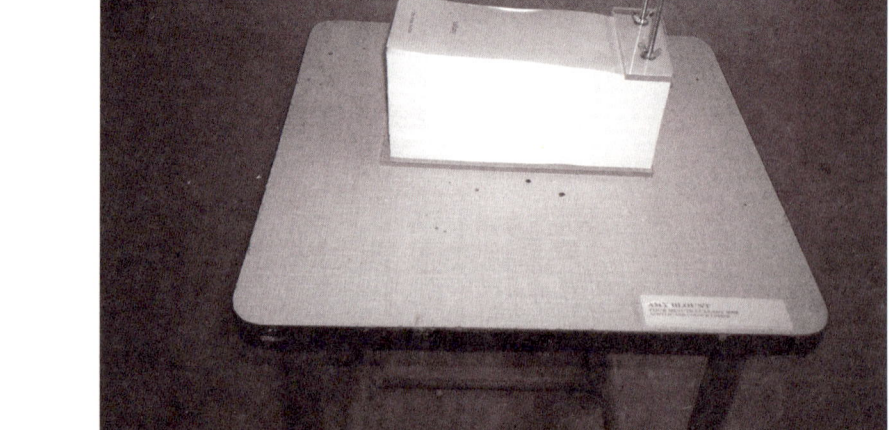

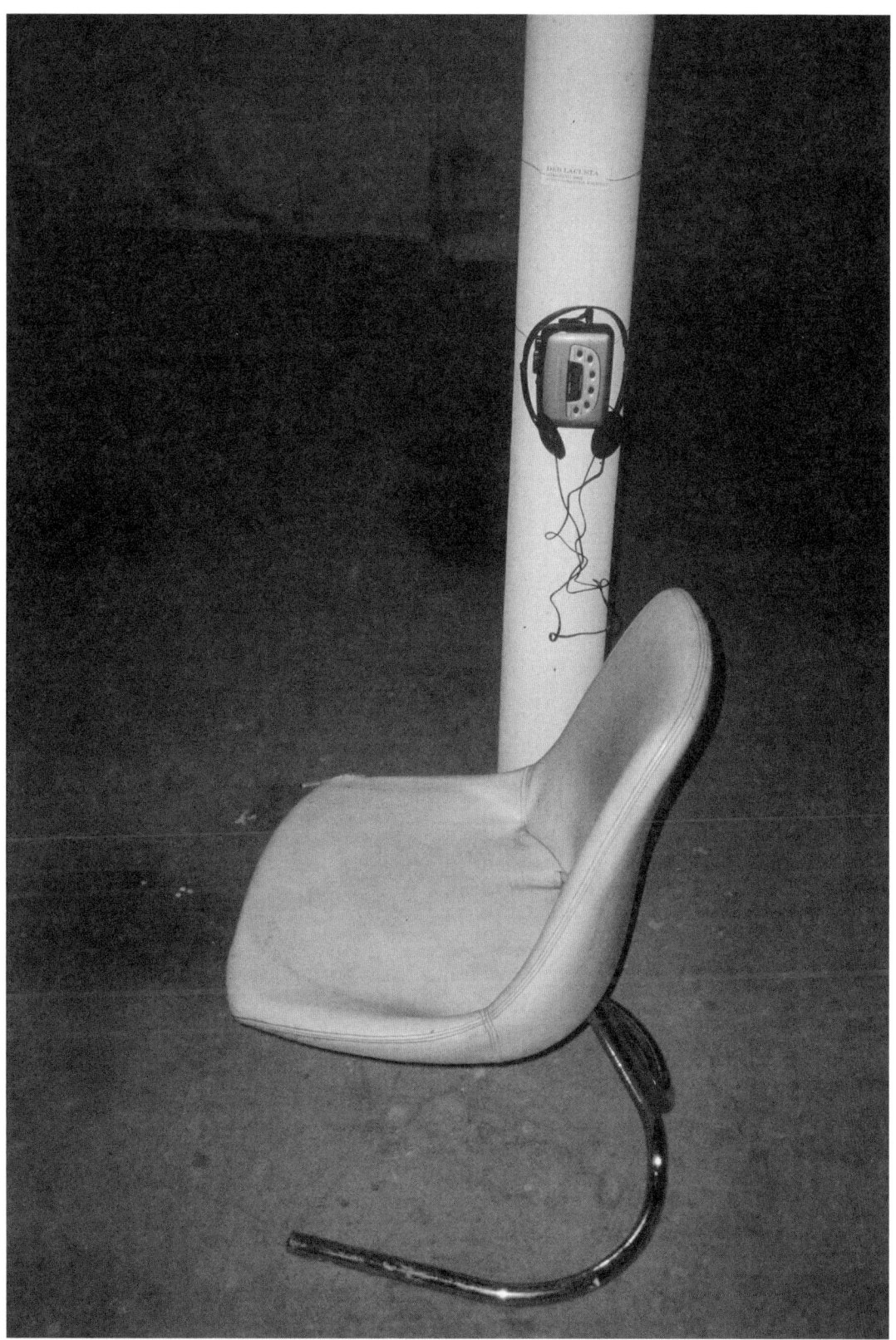

Deb Lacusta
*Miss Sing*
2001
Audio cassette and walkman
13 x 7.5 cm

The London Suitcase in L.A. with message from
Kevin Francis Gray

Clockwise from top left: Bob and Robert Smith, Seb Patane, Mark Aerial Waller, Jess Search, Luke Gottelier and Kevin Francis Gray, David Panos, Alex Valmarana and Leigh McCarthy, Tom McCarthy and Anja Büchele, Frank Hannon, Luke Milne and Jennifer Higgie, Francis Upritchard and Kate MacGarry

@ The Practice Space
5443 W. Pico
Los Angeles, CA 90010
ACROSS THE POND
February 8 - 23
Reception: Friday 8th February 7-10 PM
Open Saturday 11-6 PM or by Appointment
310.384.0982 or 310.406.0452
ZEYAD DEJANI RUNA ISLAM THERESE STOWELL
GRAHAM HUDSON & DAVE HOYLAND
JESSICA VOORSANGER BOB & ROBERTA SMITH
KEVIN FRANCIS GREY & LUKE GOTTELIER
CHRISTINE WOLFE JOHNNY GUNSHENAN
ROBIN FORSTER & JAMES BARRETT
DIANN BAUER DAVID LOCK SMALLTOWN
AL/CHARLOTTE CULLINAN & JEANINE RICHARDS
CLARE CEPRYNSKI SHAHIN AFRASSIABI
Curated by LEIGH MCCARTHY WWW.SUITCASESHOW.COM


LOS ANGELES

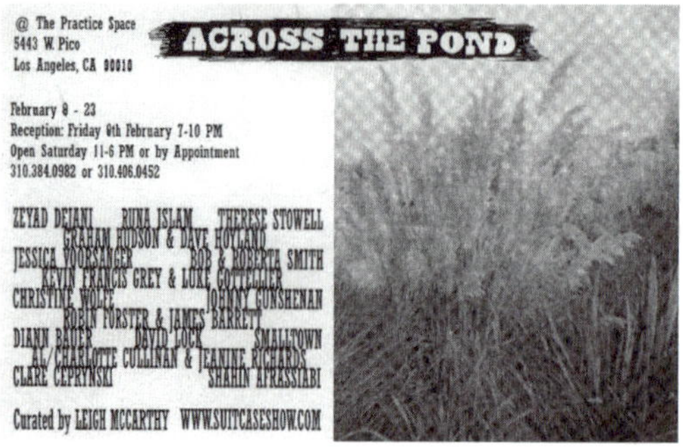

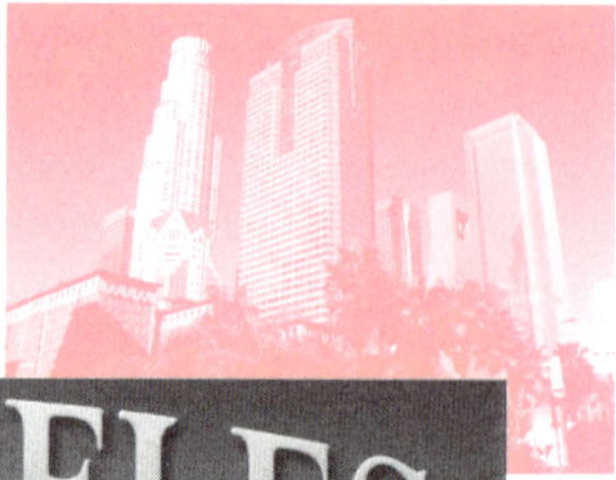

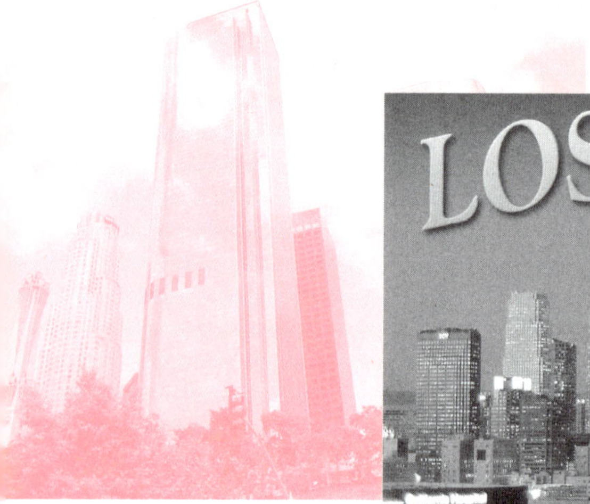

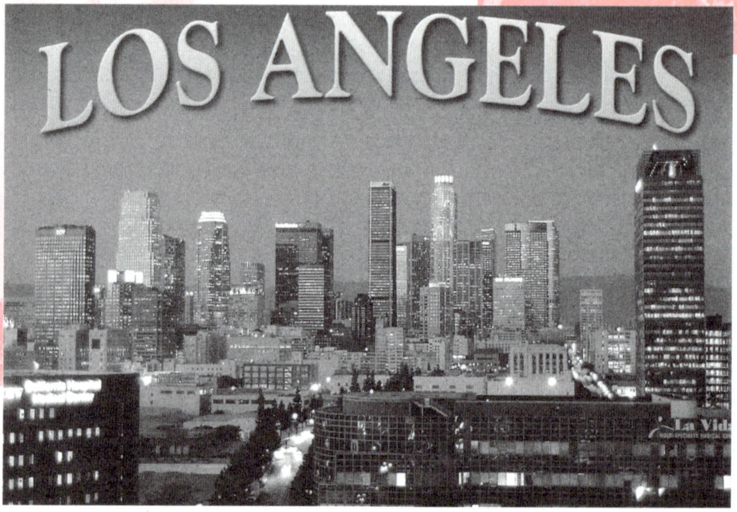

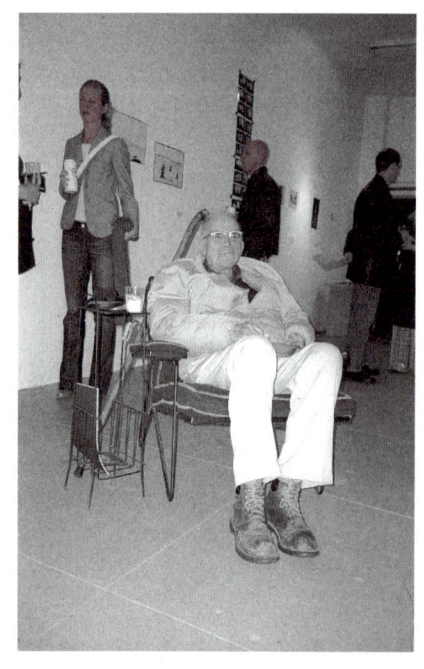

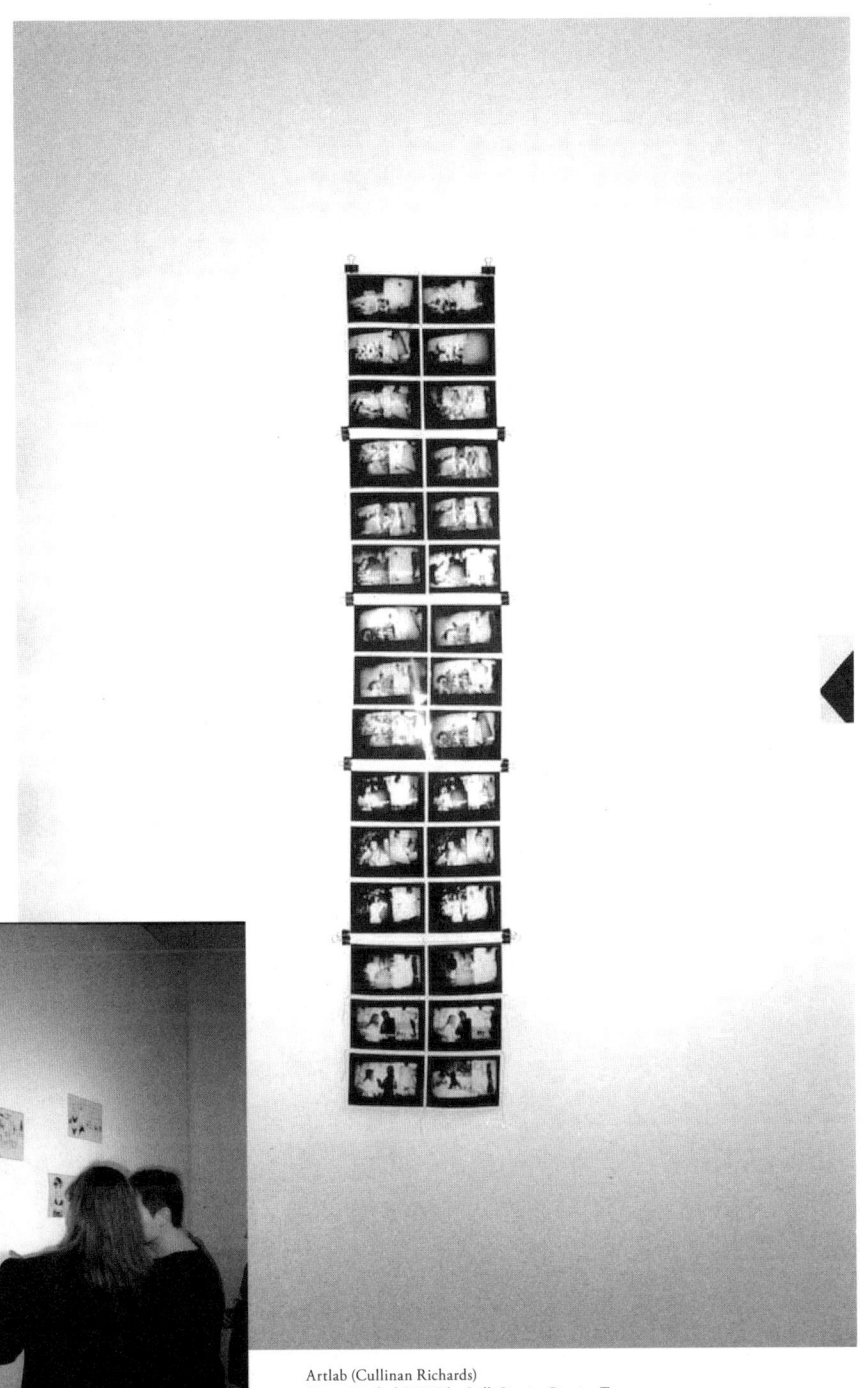

Artlab (Cullinan Richards)
*Pirate Stitched B\W Film Stills Singing Ringing Tree*
2002
B/W photographs, machine stitching
114 x 25 cm

Diann Bauer
*Untitled*
2002
Ink on tracing paper
20 x 25 cm

Leigh McCarthy
*Just the Way You Are*
2002
Video

Single Copies
(incl. postage)  . . . . . . . . . . . . . . . $1.50
Annual Subscription
(6 issues, incl. postage)    . . . . . **$8**

PERIODICAL #3.
SPRINGG
2002 £1.00

Mark Pearson
*Der Rosenkavalier*
2002
Timber, gloss paint
Dimensions variable

'The Necessary Enemy'

(0) Peter Lynch, 'Little by Little the Hand will be Revealed', 2002, oil on Canvas
(1) Debbie Lawson, 'Her Name was Lola", 2002, mixed media
(2) John Spiteri, 'Can't Do That', 2002, Video
(3) Jeremy Deadman, 'Fear', 2002, Vinyl Transfer
(4)–(11) Nicholas Stewart, 'Adventures of Robinson K.' 2002, C-Type prints
(4) 'Shitwrecked' (5) 'Provishuns cego' (6) 'Faust/Part One' (7) 'Lob (A)' (8) 'Lob (B)' (9) 'Keyhole' (10) 'Terror Firma' (11) 'outside' (Left to right)
(12) Brian Griffiths, 'Return of the Noble', 2002, mixed media
(13) Peter Lynch, 'Last Chance to Paradise', 2001, oil on Canvas
(14) Simon Bill,
(15) Peter Lynch, 'I've Done it Again', 2002, oil on Canvas
(16) Jeremy Deadman, 'Daisy', 2001, Vinyl Transfer
(17) Jeremy Deadman, 'Out of Sorts', 2001, Vinyl Transfer
(18) Peter Lynch, 'How Beautiful Can I be', 2001, oil on Canvas
(19) Debbie Lawson, '(unstable) Table', 2001, mixed media
(20) Simon Bill,
(21) Jeremy Deadman, 'Two Minute Frequency', 1998/2002, radio casing, sound
(22) Simon Bill,
(23) Simon Bill,
(24) Simon Bill,
(25) Simon Bill,
(26) Simon Bill,
(27) Mark Pearson, 'Der Rosenkervalier', 2002, mixed media
(28) Peter Lynch, 'Peckham Rye', 2001, oil on Canvas
(29) Jeremy Deadman, 'A Bloody Business', 2002, Vinyl Transfer
(30) David Thorpe and Brian Griffiths, 'We Live A Life of Endless Pleasure', 2002, Video
(31) Jeremy Deadman, 'Blinded', 2001, Vinyl Transfer

Jeremy Deadman drawing the exhibition guide

# BRIAN GRIFFITHS INTERVIEWED BY MARTIN HERBERT

David Thorpe and Brian Griffiths
*We Live a Life of Endless Pleasure*
2002
Video

MH: What might be the psychological upshots of that process, both for the viewer and for yourself?

: Over the years you've worked with cardboard constructions, used furniture, and more recently – as in *Life is a Laugh* on a London Underground platform – arrangements of objects such as a 1970s caravan, used mattresses, a heap of sand, a bicycle and a hugely oversized model of a panda's head. What determines your choice of materials?

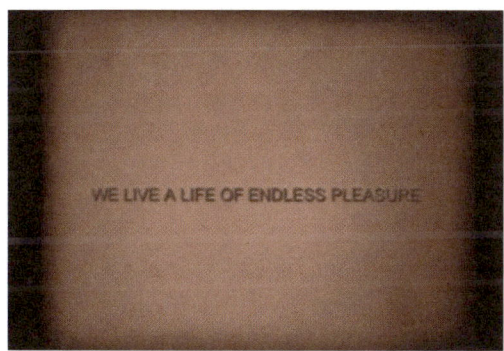

BRIAN GRIFFITHS: I'm interested in things, objects from the world. I collect things, not materials, and these become a vocabulary, a rather large and cumbersome palette. These objects are caressed or forced into becoming artworks, or parts of artworks, or bits of installations. All the works to some extent are assemblages. I'm constantly considering parts and how they meet, how they fit, the gaps – the means of holding things together. So, like any collector, I'm fascinated by accumulating, categorizing, presenting.

BG: Often I consider it as a need to escape, a repeated and heroic attempt to leave the here and now and to be transported to other places, other times and by extension, other psychological states. I need to escape from Brian Griffiths, who lives in south London, is rather short, and goes to the launderette. But I also see the artwork as a way of interrupting a space by complicating the ride from A to B – like a long discussion about a shortcut. My constructing implies the dreamer or overzealous hobbyist: this somehow just becomes another way of calling attention to the diversions we construct to feel alive.

MH: Do you have, or do you feel that your work takes up an ethical position in relation to these "diversions we construct to feel alive"?

Debbie Lawson
*(Unstable) Table*
2001
Mixed media
60 x 50 x 50 cm

*Her Name was Lola*
2002
Mixed media
400 x 45 x 45 cm

Next double spread:
Brian Griffiths
*The Return of the Noble*
2002
Wood (various), plastic,
coconut mat,
fabric, leather, polish
205 x 200 x 255 cm
Courtesy Vilma Gold, London

Simon Bill
*Looped in the Loops*
2001
Day-glo spray, emulsion and
polystyrene relief on MDF
127 x 97 x 5 cm
Courtesy Patrick Painter,
Los Angeles

Peter Lynch
*I've Done it Again*
Oil on canvas
2002
150 x 100 cm

BG: I believe that life is a network of diversions (I say, as I go and make yet another coffee). The work is a set-up – it asks for a suspension of disbelief but does not expect it, it won't offer enlightenment, it is in itself a diversion. This awareness seems important to me, and the work often seeks to set up diverse but particular kinds of investigations for the audience which implicitly or explicitly play with this idea. For example, in *The Only Living (or Your Lonely Saucer Eyes)* at the A Foundation in Liverpool, there was a grand wooden construction called *The Kingdom of the Cursed and Broken*. Because it's a container, a large cuboid, you're uncontrollably pushed around looking for the "way in" – but every apparent opening is an illusion or a blunt deadend. The destination is the journey. That entire show was a kind of expectation-builder, an exercise in growing awareness and atmosphere, where things got consistently larger yet the spectacular was undercut by an increasing blankness. There was something utterly gratuitous and wonderfully excessive … which I find funny.

MH: In the light of your interest in misdirection, then, how seriously might we be intended to take your statement "Life Is A Laugh"?

BG: The title was intended as a concise statement – one that, via posters, would be repeated around the London Underground network, butting up against crowded train windows. It was designed to live alongside the cacophony of printed matter in that environment. But as one reads, and rereads, it softly shifts into a question. There's no answer here, just an attempt to describe a situation. I think to laugh and to be happy is a lifetime project.

MH: In some ways, a work like that seems a long way from the cardboard figures and environments you first became known for, which is approximately where you were when you worked with Bart Wells Institute and organised the show *The Necessary Enemy*. Can we track back to that moment? What are your memories of that experience?

BG: I'd known Luke Gottelier and Francis Upritchard for some time, in fact I studied with Luke in Hull in the early Nineties. This made the invitation and the process of putting together a show a real pleasure. It became the classic artist-run space show of friends and tangential acquaintances, with various artists and friends generously helping out with the ad hoc installation and preparations for the opening party. The dilapidated, large, three storey building with its shabby grandeur was the starting point, and the somewhat over-acting leading player for the show.

It was a rather homespun horror – things were haunted and possessed – and it became a series of staged moments to be bumped into via dark stairwells and creaky floor boards. It was low budget, amateur and DIY, like your dad doing bad magic at a Halloween party.

MH: The theatricality inherent in your work was obviously a factor there. Superficially though, you appeared to make a concerted turn away from the cardboard aesthetic at one point; what were the factors that occasioned the shift?

BG: I wanted to extend my travels – to wear different fancy dress if you like, and to put away the *Blue Peter* suit. On one level though, I don't see the work I've made since as radically different. A marked move in recent years has been to produce installations and shows that, unlike the cardboard computer series, don't rely on a single language. There was a need in these early works to create a consistent and believable parallel world. But in recent shows there's been a desire to shift genres, materials, scale, types of constructing; to juxtapose the sculptures using found objects next to created "found" objects; and to bring together groups of sculptures to create misdirected adventures, surreal or metaphysical landscapes. I've constantly rethought this notion of the audience and how they participate, and how they can be directed and manipulated.

MH: There's a quality to these larger works that increasingly resembles stage sets for the viewer to move within. Can you characterize your work's relationship to the theatrical and, perhaps, its additional relationship to art's current interest in the "performative"?

BG: I started as a painter and was so disappointed at the time people spent looking at the paintings that I made large scale objects that would have to be navigated around. It was a desperate statement, "try and ignore this." I guess this was my first "performative" piece. Encouraging the viewer to undertake a physical action. From the early cardboard consoles I've always implicated the viewer. This was done on the most obvious level of the human scale of the objects and their functional positioning within the given space. It asked for the viewer to play a role and the materials and mode of construction heightened this. I wanted to keep things light.

MH: So is the gallery, for you, a kind of surrogate stage?

BG: *The Only Living* ... was put together for the viewer as an unfolding of space, materials and forms that uses in part theatrical devices as a way of building expectation and prolonging the viewing experience. Your movement around these still objects and the A Foundation building itself was orchestrated. By contrast the *Life Is A Laugh* installation set the challenge to produce a sculptural work that couldn't be navigated around and therefore denied investigation in a traditional sculptural manner. The platform really took on the conventions of a stage – set apart from the real. This I wanted to exploit, to create stage left and stage right, particular lighting etc. But simultaneously I wanted to soften the artwork into the real – to bring the place and artwork into the same ground – so it became the set of a building works or a forgotten storage area.

MH: In terms of this freedom of movement, your works allow a generous degree of autonomy, but also often combine a kind of grandness and fantastical quality with a very human element of failure.

BG: I don't want to create a hard-nosed complete environment, like a film set. To some extent my works function like prompts or cues for imaginative leaps, inviting a tagging-together of all kinds of cultural and personal references. The objects are often invested with something of the monumental, the grand. This imbues them with a purpose without ever quite defining it. For this reason I frequently use archetypes, the generic or the straightforward. The panda head in *Life is a Laugh* is disarmingly direct, but it attempts to grapple with sculptural art history and other stuff from the world (public sculpture, architectural entertainment or promotional objects). Somehow it becomes a strategy of making things seem matter of fact – incongruously at home, so to speak. The fantastical often points towards the historical, and therefore flirts with the outmoded or stereotypical – it rubs against the secondhandness of the "exotic" or the "foreign."

MH: Presumably your habits as a collector feed into this?

BG: For me collecting has become one important way of understanding the world. I consider this curiosity as a strategy to see your way out of a place. As a collector a kind of research is undertaken and as in early Modernist enquiry the line between novelty, entertainment and important research is erased: there's a lostness. This seems to me the state of contemporary art. I believe as an artist (and as a person) one is always bumping or seamlessly gliding from grand lofty ideas to considering the minor, and the two are often confused. The work, I always think, has high aspirations for itself that can't be met: I put together an orchestrated and measured failure. I'm fascinated by failure in all its guises – failure is something we all do well.

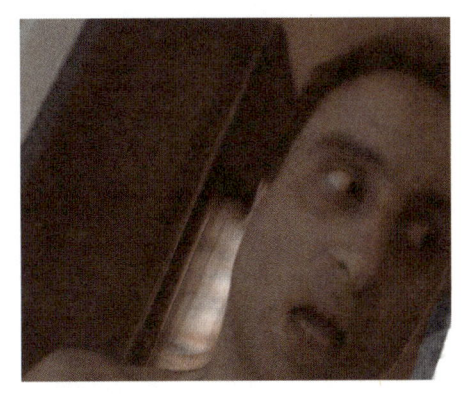

Main image:
Nicholas Stewart
*Adventures of Robinson K.*
2002
C-prints

Smaller images:
John Spiteri
*Can't Do That*
2002
Video

From left to right:

Simon Bill,
*The Fitness Exchange*
2001
Emulsion, oil and spettragel on MDF

*Tot*
2001
Acrylic and emulsion on MDF
(destroyed)

*Caligula*
2001
Oil on plywood

*The Japs*
2001
Emulsion, undercoat and gloss on MDF

Simon Bill
*Duck/Rabbit*
2000
Papier-mâché

All paintings are
127 x 97 x 5 cm
Courtesy Patrick Painter,
Los Angeles

ANNUAL
SUBSCRIPTION
OF 6 ISSUES
SIX.

£5.00

£5.00

ANNUAL

# May it Return in Spades

PERIODICAL 2002

11:49 #4

**ART WELLS INSTITUTE**

Matt Bryans, Henry Coleman,
Milena Dragicevic, Johnny Gunshenan,
Kevin Francis Gray, Frank Hannon, Art Lab,
David Noonan, Stewart Purdy,
Pet Car Returns, Simon Woolham

A Buildings
[...]don Lane
[Lon]don E8

Private View, Friday 21 June, 6.30-11PM.
Open Saturday and Sunday 12-6, 22 June-21 July,
Or by Appointment, 07903335357.
TheBartWells@Hotmail.com
Curated by Johnny Gunshenan
Design Hanoi/Gun Concepts

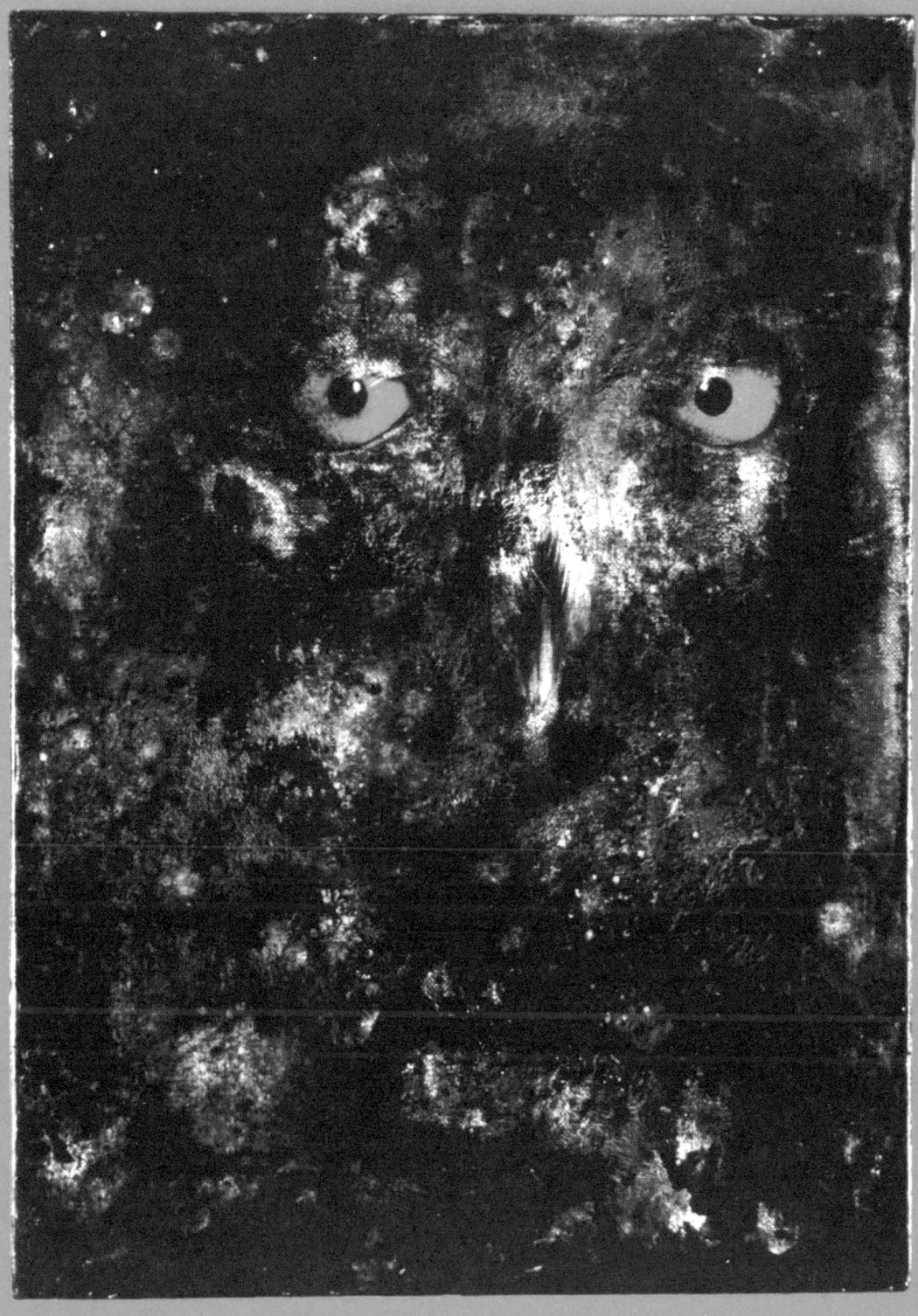

David Noonan
*Owl*
2002
Oil on canvas
38.5 x 29 cm
Courtesy Uplands Gallery, Melbourne

Artlab (Cullinan Richards)
*Trophy Wife*
2001
Paint, canvas, wood, vellum, lego
Dimensions variable

Johnny Gunshenan
*Frogs do Fractions*
2002
Texter, pen and ink on paper
200 x 120 cm

Kevin Francis Gray
*Untitled*
2002
Glitter and glue on paper
(detail)

# FRANCIS

# UPRITCHARD INTERVIEWED BY ÅBÄKE

: Dear Francis, we met quite recently, especially if we consider we could have come accross each other ten years ago when we visited Bart Wells for the first time, then a second etc. The gallery we discovered by chance, walking around our neighbourhood on a Saturday morning. It was very much a unique chance encounter as the dodgy mews your gallery was in always looked too dark, too dangerous, too close to the story of the body parts found in a suitcase by London Fields. I am not saying the area has become Switzerland but gentrification did its bit since and anybody visiting the place now wouldn't necessarily understand the bravery we showed on that day, turning left on Mare Street instead of securely continuing our route on the main road. There it was, in the corner, a derelict building untouched by any notion of health and safety, proudly showing a hastily written sign on MDF hanging above the door. I immediately liked the name as the yellow little men called the Simpsons were making me laugh and what Orson Welles had achieved with his *War of the Worlds* radio programme had always fascinated me. Of course, you told me years later the references were wrong but they were mine and it is why we entered. I might be wrong but it was damp, dark, windy and wet inside as much as outside. It was as exciting as going to Disneyland but without anybody around, if that makes sense.

I realise this was supposed to be a question: sorry. Did you live in the gallery? Did you have water, electricity, toilets, did you have to read the *Squatters Handbook*?

FRANCIS UPRITCHARD: I didn't live there at the beginning. Luke and I wanted to do a show together, but no one would have us, so we started looking for an alternative space. I was walking through the back streets with my then husband Jamie, hungover I recall, and since hungover and in that exact area I deduce we were probably looking for Vietnamese food. I like crab/corn soup when I'm hungover. Anyway, we went past this open door, and being curious poked our heads in. We were a bit scared that some scary persons might live there, so we tentatively explored … lots of needles and the like littering the litter, but there was no one there, so I went and bought a one pound lock and locked the front door. A week later it was still locked, so Luke and I decided to clean it a little and do a show there. At that point we got a really expensive lock! Cleaning mostly involved getting rid of masses of cardboard and shovelling a disgusting amount of bird poo. When I listen to the Strokes I want to throw up, because it reminds me of pigeons. Oh and water and electrics were turned on. Toilets were pretty good too. The *Squatters Handbook* was too long, so I didn't bother. Later, after my husband and I parted ways, I moved into the top floor but that was perhaps a year after the gallery opened. Did you and Kajsa come to one of our parties or just one day when it was open? I seem to remember you saying you came to *May it Return in Spades* which opened with a big party with bands and all, and that's when a lot of people came the first time. Oops, am I interviewing you now?

Å: We went twice inside but during daytime. One of the shows was the one with the stag furniture sculpture by Brian Griffiths and another one with newspaper drawings on the windows. Was that the same show? I seem to recall seeing one of the parties going on but we were too shy to enter as we didn't know anybody then. What year are we talking about here?

I am not going to ask you whether you were aware of other artist-run places in the area but perhaps focus on the food. Have you always been this interested in self-growing vegetables or food in general? Did you have an allotment then?

FU: We are talking about 2002 and 3. I think. I have a terrible memory. The bits of cut paper was Johnny Gunshenan's curated show called *May it Return in*

*Spades* and you were looking at a Matt Bryans' installation. It was on this crumbly brick wall and very beautiful. As for Brian's work ... he made a Don Quixote-type character with some type of mule.

I have always been interested in food, growing it has come recently ... mum grew most of our vegetables when we were young, so when I started with the allotment, which was at the same time as Bart Wells, I half remembered how to grow things. At Bart Wells we often had crumpets and tea up by the open fire on the top floor, which we ran pretty constantly in winter to keep warm. At the openings sometimes we had gas heating – the gas was donated by the Maltese developer in the next building from us. He was very sweet to us, but did find us quite confusing. One day he came to see me and saw I was cold and sent one of his workers over with a hundred quid and a note saying "buy a jumper."

Back to food ... at one opening we had really delicious sausages and buns cooked by a chef friend Megan Jones. We probably did more food stuff, but my memory ... I'll ask Luke. Luke and I met over food – at a dinner party in Regents Studios (in those days Ada St. Studios) and we realised that we lived near each other and both liked cooking, so we'd cook for one another. Later we realised that we really liked each other's work and were into the same kind of art. At that time Luke and I were about the same level at cooking ... but then Luke started working at Moro, did his supper club with Kevin Francis Gray, and got quite obsessed about cooking so now his food is just amazing. I first met Johnny at an 18 course meal Luke and Kevin cooked.

I on the other hand got obsessed with eating! My sister Hannah doesn't really care much about food ... she'll eat anything and will be happy about it – I don't really understand that.

This page and next double spread:
Matt Bryans
*Untitled*
2002
Erased newspaper cuttings
Dimensions variable
Courtesy Kate MacGarry, London

Frank Hannon
*Untitled*
2002
Pencil and ink on wood
28 x 40 cm

Milena Dragicevic
*Monument*
2000
Oil on canvas
41cm x 36cm

*Gatati*
2002
Oil on linen
67cm x 52cm

Stuart Purdy
*MM*
2002
Acrylic on canvas
66 x 51cm

# ARE YOU DANCIN'? ARE YOU ASKIN'?

# THE BART WELLS INSTITUTE MUSIC PROGRAMME

It seems so long ago now. But it's what – only seven, eight years? Try as I might to form them into a representative picture, my memories of the two gigs I played at the Bart Wells Institute are like scuffed, torn and scattered dance cards: fragments that index conversations, moments of abandon, fights, social embarrassments and simple, happy enthusiasms. Any narrative adhesion has long been rotted away by too many years of too many late nights; my recollections are at best like grotty coagulations of dirt or puddles of depotentiated chemicals. The chances of me forming them into anything like a useful account are non-existent. This will have to be tendentious and partisan. But I can at least start with a few facts.

I used to play in a band called Norwegian Lady. The band comprised one writer (me), three artist-musicians (Dave Carbone, Thom Driver and Jared Fisher), one artist-turned-adman (Phil McCluney) and a computer scientist (Arran Derbyshire). We were a motley bunch, barely sharing the same musical tastes let alone musical ability. But something between us clicked and our lack of shared sensibility somehow resulted in the band being able to create an absurdist, disco-rock grotesquery that, if nothing else, made us and a few other people laugh and smile a great deal. For the four years of Norwegian Lady's life, we bashed out our shonky songs on a logistically troublesome battery of ancient synthesizers, guitars and toy instruments at some of London's stinkiest toilet venues and ad hoc art galleries.

The band met through various acquaintances on London's art scene and, as such, the majority of our gigs tended to be in small, artist-run spaces around Hackney, where we played to small audiences of friendly faces. Our first gigs, in 2001, were truly awful; it was as if a curse had been placed upon us by some malevolent God of Rock we'd angered in a previous musical life. Amps would fuse. Keyboards would mysteriously stop working. We'd be too drunk or terrified to remember our parts. On one particularly abject occasion, someone urinated on the wooden floor above the room we were playing in, causing the lights to go and a gentle waterfall of piss to cascade all over us as we tried to play in total darkness. Far from being the stuff of rock'n'roll legend, these early gigs were mortifying experiences, compounded only by the two socially-challenged drummers we went through before Dave took up sticks for us; one an American with the implausible name of Kent Boxer who at one point claimed he was living in a park then suddenly disappeared back to the States; the other a pumped-up, monomaniacal control freak called Colin, my memories of whom have been repressed by what I can only assume is a form of post-traumatic stress syndrome. At the start of 2002 we were on the verge of chucking the band in, but we instead decided to give the Lady a break for a few months in order to rethink the whole sorry endeavour. It was around this time that the Bart Wells gang first crow-barred open the doors of their Institute and in July 2002 Norwegian Lady were invited to play there on the closing night of the exhibition *May It Return In Spades*, curated by Johnny Gunshenan (better known by his stage name, Johnny Vivash). So, we took a deep breath, scrapped our luckless old songs in favour of an entirely new set, and decided that Norwegian Lady should take her chances just off Mare Street, behind a bunch of Vietnamese supermarkets, at 3 Silesia Buildings.

A tattered flyer for the event tells me that there was 'Food by Megan and Donna' and that the following bands played that night: Norwegian Lady, Some Product, Pillow Fight, Mark Corcoran, The Annoying Cowboys, Adrian R. Teenbeat, Snakes and Matt. But this is where it starts to get hazy. With memory jogged by my fellow ex-Norwegian Lady members, I can tell you that:

1. It was a hot summer evening and the Bart Wells was sticky, sweaty and rammed by the time we played, which was late into the night. It also smelled strongly of grilled food, from Megan and Donna's smoky indoor barbecue in the room above.

2. We played on the ground floor and the ceiling sloped and warped alarmingly as people made their way about whilst we played. There was no stage and the audience was just a few feet away from us.

3. Adrian R. Teenbeat's music reminded me of a cross between John Shuttleworth and The Fall – a kind of loose, garage rockabilly sound tempered with a certain deprecatory melancholy (I may be confusing this memory with seeing him play on another occasion.)

4. Playing the Bart Wells that night was one of the most enjoyable gigs in Norwegian Lady's existence and one that gave the group a new lease of life. Our gear didn't malfunction! We played new songs and people danced! People cheered! The crowd even wanted an encore!

5. The band before Norwegian Lady, Snakes (which featured members of the group Antifamily, Jamie King, David Panos and Benedict Seymour, along with artist Nick Brooks), were far better than we were. Musically tight and cerebral, Snakes had a heavy, muscular guitar sound and played as if trained by some highly adept American hardcore band, such as Shellac or Black Flag. I remember wondering whether I'd be able to get away with reading lyrics out of a book as Snakes' singer did on their final song (was it poetry? Political theory?), but thinking better of it.

6. After the gig, some drunken fool started throwing bricks at a bus parked outside the Bart Wells. One of the bricks missed the bus but smashed the windscreen of Luke Gottelier's Peugeot 205, which was parked behind it. Luke confronted the drunk, telling him to stop and a tussle ensued between them. The fight was stopped with the calm words "OK boys, break it up" from Norwegian Lady's implacable guitarist Jared. It's hard to believe Norwegian Lady were both the entertainment and security for the evening.

The second time we played at Bart Wells was the following winter. It was bitterly cold, and there was no heating in the space, save for in the kitchen/living area right at the top of the building, where Luke fed us stew before the gig. I remember even less about this night than the first. We played in the same spot on the ground floor as before, but this time the bands were surrounded by metal chains hanging from the ceiling which were part of Goshka Macuga's *Salon*, and which made each group look as if they were playing in some kind of gallery-turned-S&M dungeon. Phil Duckworth and Ben Sadler of Juneau Projects played at some point earlier in the evening, under the wonderfully apt name Art School Graduate. The set involved the two, both dressed as Father Christmas, bouncing around to splenetic mutant hip-hop in an almost schizophrenic transformation from their previous incarnation as shy, thoughtful, post-rock outfit Ohne. I can't recall the name of the band just before Norwegian Lady, but I do remember it was our drumkit being used that evening, and that the drummer in the group before us had whacked the snare drum so hard during their interminably long set, that he split the drum head open. His lack of contrition and the evident belief on that band's part that smashing someone else's gear was a mark of musical innovation sparked a row between us, but one that failed to escalate into anything worse due to the fact that it was far too cold to stand around arguing with each other.

Broken drums aside, my abiding memory of the whole evening – much like my memory of the Bart Wells project in general – is largely the sense of being part of a community. It sounds almost mawkish to say so, but such is the lack of any documentation of the gigs that feelings are all I have to go on here. I could bang on like some tedious ageing rocker about the shambolic but spirited energy of the gigs at Bart Wells. I could continue with reminiscences about Norwegian Lady, but it's a band long dead and only one of the many that played at Bart Wells. It would also be easy to wax far too romantic about the Institute's semi-legality, about its DIY approach to exhibition-making, about the way ventures like these are co-opted by The Man and steamrollered by local gentrifiers. But getting all misty-eyed might undermine the fact that the bands that passed through the Institute's doors were made to feel that music had an important role amongst this group of artists. As musicians we felt valued not as some kind of variety act invited merely to spice up an exhibition opening (as is so often the case) but that we were contributing to the social cohesion of a local artist community. At times like these, with so much uncertainty in the air and in a city as large as London – a city in which you can drown beneath waves of social or economic forces – the importance of places such as the Bart Wells Institute is not to be underestimated.

— Dan Fox

This issue:

JOHNNY GUNSHIMAN      ARTLAB

KEVIN FRANCIS GRAY     MATT BRYANS
                       HENRY COLEMAN

FRANK HANNON          MILENA DRAGICEVIC

STUART PURDY          DAVID NOONAN

SIMON WOOLHAM

£5.00 FOR 1 YEAR'S SUBSCRIPTION

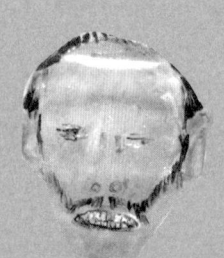

TO: 3 Silex Buildings
London
E6

# BART WELLS INSTITUTE PICTORIAL

£ 1

NUMBER 5  SUMMER 2002

3 Silesia Buildings, London E8

Flyer designed by Pablo Picasso ©2002
any similarity to Julian Opie is coincidential. small print  small print   small print

# viva Pablo

**Private View:**
Friday 2nd August 2002
7pm till 10pm
The Bart Wells Institute is at:
3 Silesia Buildings E8
(off London Lane)
Nearest tube: Bethnal Green
(then bus d6, 106, or 253)
Open every saturday and sunday
from 12-6 (or by appointment).
Show closes Sunday 8th of Sept.
For more information...
Phone: 07715778017
Email harry_pye@hotmail.com

**Featureing more than 30 previously unseen Pablo works from the years 1973 to 2002 on loan from the private collections of;**
Gordon Beswick, Matt Calderwood,
Billy Childish, Chris Coombes,
Dan Connor, Elidh Crumlish, Stuart Cumberland,
Johnny de Veras, Luke Gottelier, Liz Haarala,
Peter Harris, Mat Humphrey, Mark Jackson,
Jasper Joffe, Geoff lucas, Karen Morden &
Paul Hamilton, John Moseley, Andrew Mottershead,
Paul Munn, Humphrey Ocean, Chris Owen,
Olivia Plender, The Pye Family, Kes Richardson,
Cuong Sam, Ed Scotland, Veronica Seifert &
Cordelia Underhill, Adrian R. Shaw,
Anna Sheppard & Janet Hamilton-Gill,
Adam Shepherd, Rowland Smith, Anik Todd,
Francis Upritchard, Edward Ward,
Richard Wathen, Kit Wise

## BART WELLS INSTITUTE

*Pablo's Sleeping Bag* by Anna Shepherd
and Janet Hamilton Gill from Picasso's
"bisexual period"

Edward Ward
*The Pablo*
2002
Pen, ink and watercolour on paper
29.7 x 21 cm

# METRO LIFE

*Picasso's Flirtations: Three Figures At The Base Of The Crucifixion (After Bacon) by Veronica Seifert and Cordelia Underhill*

# Picasso lives

### ART REVIEW
Viva Pablo

The Bart Wells Institute is a great name for setting up expectations. What you'll find, though, is an almost derelict house in Hackney, at the end of a block covered by a curtain of plastic and undergoing serious renovation work.

It's just as well, then, that they manage to put on some lively and idiosyncratic exhibitions. The premise for this one is simple: just imagine if Picasso hadn't died in 1973 and had continued to produce work influenced by artists working today. So what if he had fallen on hard times, slumming it in the Elephant And Castle and New Cross and teaching primary school kids in Lewisham?

Put together by off-beat curator Harry Pye, here we're offered the results of Picasso's flirtations with David Hockney, the Ska revival and BritArt. The latter is Tracey Emin (actually by Anna She— and Janet Hamilton-Gill), and a pa— of a Chris Ofili-type canvas (F— Upritchard) that, instead of standi— Ofili's characteristic mounds of el— dung, stands on two bread rolls, co— with small bread sticks arranged li— fat bread fingers in the famous phot— of the artist.

Featuring contributors such as — Stuckist Billy Childish (who's pai— cubist Kylie) and designers from the w— Web and set design, you may have — guessed this is not a serious counter— exercise, but rather a child's play-box — ideas. But what else could you expec— you are promised the Spice Girls po— Les Demoiselles d'Avignon?   *Fisu*—

*Until Sept 8, The Bart Wells Institute, 3— Buildings (off Mare Street) E8, Sat and — midday to 6pm, free. Tel: 07762 363 6— Tube: Bethnal Green.*

---

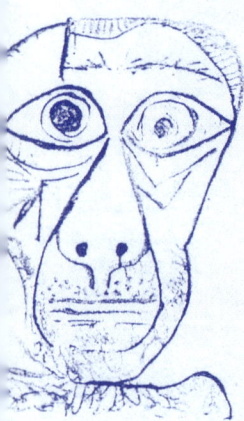

ELLS INSTITUTE
uildings, off London Lane,
Pablo Curator Harry Pye's
of artworks live up to their
ns in that they are attributed
on the premise he didn't die
t instead moved to South
nd has carried on working
ast 30 years influenced by the
culture of the times.
texts explaining the work in
icasso's Two Tone period,
eriod and Viagra Period,
ers are a Chris Ofili-style
painting showing Nelson
celebrating his freedom and a
yle portrait of the Spice Girls.
4 Aug. Ends Sun 8 Sep.

, Luke Gottelier, Stuart
nd (painting, *pictured*)
s of others make the
Picasso might have
ad he been alive during
d years – including his
Period' and 'Brit Art
iva Pablo' is at the
Institute until
r 8. See East End

DON | August 28-September 4

Stuart Cumberland
*Picasso Portrait in Black*
2001
Acrylic on canvas
55 x 46 cm

# HARRY PYE INTERVIEWED BY LUKE GOTTELIER

HARRY PYE: I found this the other day (cf. p. 77 – 78). It's a letter Francis Upritchard sent. In my memory, she wrote "We've just found this space, a squat that we're going to turn into a gallery" but of course in reality she doesn't say that at all. The letter is all about this terrible accident she'd had and the damage it had done to her face. The main reason I ended up saying yes to being in the exhibition *The Bart Wells Gang* was because I felt so bad about her being wounded and scarred. I couldn't really say no.

LUKE GOTTELIER: So the letter doesn't actually mention Bart Wells Institute at all?

HP: No. It must have been afterwards when we spoke on the phone that she said "we've found this space." The best part of the letter is the sketches. I've always liked her little self-portrait which includes lines explaining where the doctors are going to operate on her.

LG: I was going to ask what your first recollections of Bart Wells Institute are.

HP: I was thinking "How do I get home?" I was worried about being lost and I was a bit embarrassed with Francis coming from New Zealand and her knowing London better than I did even though I was born there. But I remember her saying you get the tube to Bethnal Green and then get a bus which took me about an hour and a half and it seemed ridiculous. I'd never heard of Mare Street or Well Street, the places she described. And then we went down an alley and everyone was on a bike apart from me, and I've never learnt to ride a bike, it's always been one of those things that if you say you don't, people think you're joking. All of a sudden she stopped and said "this is where I fell off my bike, where I had that accident." So when I got to the actual building I couldn't see the enthusiasm that you and Francis had for it. I couldn't see the dream. And also you'd spent most of the day scraping off tons of pigeon shit and because it took me so long to get there it looked like I'd made an excuse.

LG: What do you remember of the interior of the space?

HP: Really, really rundown and looking like it would fall on top of you. You could imagine it on fire and bits falling off. And it was really out of my world because I wasn't making art.

LG: At that point you were making fanzines. I'm trying to work out how we came to ask you to be in the first show. Because I'm not sure I'd seen any of your artwork at that point. You'd organised shows hadn't you?

HP: We knew each other because I was going to interview Stuart Cumberland for *Frank* magazine and he said I should interview you instead. I went to the South London Gallery and Julian Schnabel was giving a talk. Then we met on the way to the Hermit's Cave pub and when we got there you were incredibly standoffish and cold. Then I mentioned Bruce McLean and the fact that I knew him and I thought "Oh, he's suddenly paying attention."

LG: I remember very clearly meeting you, walking along Camberwell New Road. You had a carrier bag and gave me something from it. Probably a *Frank* magazine which I went home and read. I remember getting in touch and asking for more.

HP: You gave some money to Stuart Cumberland to give to me. At that time I was broke, living hand to mouth, wherever was free. But the only reason I can think of why I was so broke is that I spent the money on *Frank* magazines. Then I asked you to be in my exhibition in Paris *It May Be Rubbish But It's British Rubbish* and also *Harry Pye's Great British Art Show*. At that opening you met Kevin Francis Gray. I remember the two of you both coming up to me and thanking me for introducing you to the other one. You had this phase of swapping coats and stuff like that, sort of inseparable. In November 2000 I did a show in Soho based around William Blake's Proverbs of Hell. Mat Humphrey had been great at finding venues for a series of shows in unused shops. My William Blake show featured you, Mat and Francis. I can remember, a few months later, Francis phoning me up at the Tate and saying that you both wanted to give me a stall at Bart Wells to give out the magazines. So why I went away and did this satire on the Turner Prize …

LG: The way I remember it is that from the outset there were going to be five artists and that included you as one of the artists, but that didn't necessarily mean it would be photos or paintings or whatever, you might do an installation with the magazine or some sort of writing. Tell me more about what you had in *The Bart Wells Gang*.

HP: I had a Turner Prize acceptance speech painted in the style of Peter Davies, but using the Adrian Mitchell poem about the Vietnam War, *Tell me Lies about Vietnam*. I made it changing Vietnam to the Arts Council or Goldsmiths, things like "Rub salt into my eyes Blow pepper up my nose Stick a knife into my heart Cut off both my ears Fill a bucket with my tears AND TELL ME *LIES* ABOUT THE I.C.A. BEING A BIT SHIT." I said to Johnny de Veras that I wanted to make my acceptance speech like a Peter Davies and Johnny said he'd do it. And I was selling postcards in the Tate shop of Anthony Gormley who I've never liked. I thought "I'd like to make myself out of chicken wire." Mat Humphrey said he could do that, so we built this six foot version of me. Then Ed Ward said "Can I be in? I could do some pencil drawings of you?" I was not in a happy place and I had people like you saying you wanted me to be in shows, this guy Johnnie Bassett saying he wanted to take photos of me … it was like being the Elephant Man or something. Also, another thing that was happening around that time was that a lot of my student friends were employed by Mike Smith – whose studio makes most of the work for the Turner Prize. I thought it was all really clever and witty but if I was to do it now I would make it much more simplistic, because I don't really like work that is semi-ironic and clever. It's better to keep things simple. Can you remember much about how you first discovered Bart Wells?

LG: The first thing I remember is that Francis and her then boyfriend, Jamie King, told me to come and have a look. They'd found this building. I think that they were cycling around together, went down this shitty backstreet, saw a boarded-up building and thought "We'll have a look in here." At that time Francis and I were trying to find somewhere to do a show, and it was the classic story of speaking to galleries and galleries never being interested, so having to do it yourself. I think Jamie was the one that went in, he's got that devil-may-care attitude, who gives a fuck.

HP: He seems to have a Jeffrey Archer-type confidence. He's got this way of talking to people and being convinced we're all jolly nice chaps. Whereas most people don't get involved. I remember the first time I met him he said "You came by Old Street, were there lots of sniffer dogs?" And I said No, and he said "The police are looking for all the people who are trying to smoke drugs." I got the feeling, in the same way that you were much more knowledgable about art world things …

LG: … he was up on sniffer dogs?

Fans of Harry Pye made their own *Viva Pablo* t-shirt

HP: He was up on "know your rights," squatting. That kind of thing.

LG: The other thing I remember is how unlikely it all seemed. It was in such a state, did you see it with the stacks and stacks of cardboard everywhere? It seemed impossible that you would ever be able to do an exhibition there.

HP: When I saw it, it looked absolutely ridiculously messy. I think there were four of you there, maybe Sam Basu as well, and you'd spent all day tidying up and you were all saying "You should have seen it at half past ten" and me saying "It was WORSE?"

LG: I would always be slightly more cynical than Francis about the reason to spruce it up. Out of laziness.

HP: Francis had a confidence that I didn't at all. I remember being on a bus with Francis and her going up to men and giving them flyers in a way that when you're an outoftowner you think "What've I got to lose?" and me thinking "You don't just go up to someone and say …" I remember the private view, there were only about two people, both saying "Gosh! It's very different" and you saying "They'll come, they'll come." It seemed like a million miles from where I lived. I'd agreed to work on the bar for an hour and the second my hour was up these friends drove me straight back home and I almost wanted to kiss the road just because it was South London. Looking back it's interesting for me to see that I had very little self-confidence and had lots of trouble doing day to day things. Yet, I had no problem enlisting the help of others to do daft projects. Part of the fake Turner Prize was a rejection video – slightly inspired by things I'd seen by Douglas Gordon and Georgina Starr. Each week for a couple of months I got Gordon Beswick to film me dumping attractive women. I told them it was because I cared for them that I was ending our relationship. They deserved better etc. It was supposed to be funny and I got them to rub onions in their eyes to make them cry but often it got a bit weird and uncomfortable. Some artists believe not knowing if you've embarrassed yourself or not is a good sign. One of my heroes, Jerry Dammers, once told me the aim of the second Specials LP was to baffle the hell out of people. He wanted to have a record where no one was sure if they liked it or not. My fake Turner Prize was called *If Voting Changed Anything They'd Abolish It*. I was trying things out, testing the waters. It was a bit of a mess really. I remember laughing when a reviewer said "Pye looks like someone going for an interview for a job he's not going to get."

LG: There was a good reaction in terms of getting things in print and I remember thinking, this is the start of something big. But by the end of Bart Wells the shows weren't getting reviewed much. And the whole time we did the gallery we only sold one piece of work.

HP: Really, what was that?

LG: It was one of Francis's urns. Bought by Rut Blees Luxemburg for two hundred Euros. So let's talk about *Viva Pablo* because about seven months after that we asked you to curate a show. And we had no idea what you were going to do.

HP: I came across the Picasso quotation "Give me a gallery and I'll fill it." I've always been interested in him dying in 1973, the year I was born. Also I wanted to do a show "Art since 1978" around the time of the *I Love the Seventies* telly programme. So I put the two together and came up with the idea of Picasso faking his own death and finding 30 artists to make a work for each year since 1973. I remember thinking "This is the best idea ever!" I immediately phoned Humphrey Ocean, to get someone a bit different, a Royal Academy person, and I said "What do you think of the idea?" He said "It's pretty naff Harry, but then like all ideas it depends how you do it." Then I phoned you up and there was a pause long enough to say you weren't into it. And then I phoned up Mat Humphrey and there was another pause …

LG: I must've had enough conviction to not say "That's embarrassing, please come up with another idea" or "I've changed my mind Harry."

HP: I remember there being a change of situation where you gave me money up front.

LG: Really?

HP: You said how much will it cost you to do the flyer and gave me a hundred pounds which seemed an astonishingly large amount of money. It was such desperate times. Another thing, I wasn't allowed to make money from it. I was given a budget. Whereas before I would've potentially risked money if no one had turned up. But I think Francis said "It's not right that anyone makes money from the Bart Wells."

LG: Yeah, that was our epitaph. We made the most money selling booze from the bar at *Viva Pablo*. You had that tactic of inviting lots of artists to be in the show because the private view was absolutely rammed.

HP: I remember it being really packed. There were a couple of times at Bart Wells when the floor was moving and the staircase was rattling and you were thinking this could so easily … five hundred people crushed.

LG: It was a Health and Safety Officer's bad dream that building.

HP: At the private view Adrian Shaw played and Olivia Plender couldn't understand why a man from Barnsley would be doing a George Formby-style song with an out-of-tune guitar. It was baffling to her why anyone would clap at the end of that. Another thing that happened that hadn't happened to me at my shows in Paris or Lee Green was that Peter Davies was made reference to in the artwork and then Peter Davies would come and see the show. Who else? Matthew Collings came. I remember telling him about it in the Tate shop. He said "What a brilliant idea," the first person. And my Uncle Nick, he said it was a fantastic idea.

LG: Isn't it the same idea as Kippenberger? *The Paintings Pablo Couldn't Paint Anymore* do you know them? It's the idea that he's continuing the work, and Jacqueline Roque painted them for Picasso. I can't remember whether Kippenberger's taken over the legacy, or Jacqueline has, or maybe Picasso hasn't died. But it's a similar kind of trajectory.

HP: My references were actually things like *I Love the Eighties*.

LG: Stuart Cumberland had that great painting in it, didn't he, the last self-portrait?

HP: That was the sort of thing that should have sold for a lot of money.

LG: He's destroyed it now.

HP: It was very ghostly. He does do very good things. When they're on the money, they're really on the money. Also, I knew I could write all the blurbs on the wall.

LG: I don't remember that. Did you have Tate-style panels?

HP: We got one done in the Tate font, *Welcome to Viva Pablo*.

One of a series of paintings by Adrian R. Shaw based on Picasso's *Cat and Bird*, 1939

Rowland Smith
*Mummy, Mummy I'm a Harlequin*
2002
Oil on canvas

LG: I've always loved that, playing around with the titles next to the work or a big sign for the show. Sam Basu had that ugly Jenny Holzer sign saying "Tombs of the Fantasy Undead" endlessly. He also made signs for each artist out of lead that were completely unreadable (cf. p. 100).

HP: What other shows were there? Tell me the procession.

LG: There was Brian Griffiths' show *The Necessary Enemy*.

HP: That was powerful. He had much more of an artist's eye for displaying things. My thing was that I could come up with childlike ideas, whereas in his show the work wasn't spectacular but his brain was such a different set-up to mine. It was so impressive the way he could work out how to put these enormous works in … that actual being-a-curator thing.

LG: He took it to another level. We'd done the first show and it was a bit wonky and ramshackle and it messed around with what you expect of a show. He did something that wasn't slick, but it had a real visual drive that made it very dynamic. It really did lay down the gauntlet for everyone that followed – can you top this show?

HP: I remember thinking there was this momentum building, but not who's topping who but who's going to take the bat and whack it in another direction.

LG: I'm into this thing of putting people in that don't really go. Which is partly why you were in there at the beginning. That's why Billy Childish was there. Who's the one person you could put in who's most unlikely in a contemporary art exhibition? I get bored seeing the same people over and over again. What are your assumptions about the gang? Whose taste are you transmitting? The shows were uneven, but that was part of the interest in giving the space over to a

A painting by Harry Pye from Picasso's "expensive period"

Karen Morden and Paul Hamilton's painting from Picasso's "tangled up in blue period"

different artist each time. I hoped that by picking the right person and them knowing the space a little bit that they'd do a great show. That was the whole point, letting artists curate shows and letting them fall on their face – or pull off something great.

HP: If only someone had come and put a ballet on … or a hundred televisions back-to-back. The Bart Wells needed one other person to come in and be way more different. Maybe it needed someone to come in and do a superpristine show.

LG: I guess one of the reasons why it started to run out of steam is we just didn't have any money. All the money we made was from the bar. That limits what people can do with equipment and so on, although we always made it possible. If you don't have the money for invigilation as a starting point then it's really difficult. To be able to approach people that you think might be a bit unapproachable and say "we want you to curate a show, and we've got no money, and you'll have to do the legwork, and invigilate." It's a bit of an impossible proposal. Some people would still say yes, but it had to be people who would take the limits of the situation and make it into a virtue. Which most people did.

Mat Calderwood's sculpture inspired by
the idea of Picasso visiting South London's
Elephant and Castle

Adrian R. Shaw
*From America … to Bin Laden*
2002
Ink on paper
29.7 x 21 cm
Cover of Harry Pye's *The A to B of Culture*

Dear Harry,

I'm so jealous about your Prince Charles opertunity. Various gags that could wind you up in jail come to mind immediatly.

I'd love to come to your "why bother" night. I'm sure I'll be okay by then — but please give my apologies to Liz as I prefer to stay home and freak out about my possible surgery the next day. "on wednesday"

Here is a diagram of what they have done to me so far

— metal plate on cheek + lots of screws (inside skin)
— sticks inside mouth

here is what they want to do next:

- opening above hair line
- scar (2cm)
- metal plates + lots of screws
- more stiches inside mo[uth]

At the moment I look like this from abov[e]

← This side slightly sunken in but quite hard to tell.

So I'm really doing my head in here wondering wether to bother or not and waiting for the swelling to go down to see the 'full EXTENT!!'

Hope you like Log - as always its a weird issue. I'm sure they wont pay you for about 1 year but it will come. Thanks for doing the interview.

x Francis

please pass on the card to L[iz]

Mat Humphrey and Mark Jackson with Jackson's
*Hugh Grant's Blue Period*

*Viva Pablo* installation view

HAVE YOU SEEN THIS JUMPER? PLEASE CONTACT BART WELLS INSTITUTE 3 SILESIA BUILDINGS, LONDON E8

# ANOTHER SHITTY DAY IN PARADISE

#6 AUTUMN 2002

PHILLIP ALLEN
COLIN LOWE AND RODDY THOMSON
GIANPAOLO COTTINO
LUKE GOTTELIER
FRANCIS UPRITCHARD
BILLY CHILDISH

PRIVATE VIEW FRIDAY 20TH SEPT
SAT 21ST SEPT – SUN 3RD NOV

BART WELLS INSTITUTE

3 Silesia Buildings, London E8
2–6pm    07951 746 283

thebartwells@hotmail.com

CURAT

**Imbition**

Through job scarcity and insecurity social and environmental depravation the people I grew up with must have by now reached a level of egolessness that the Buddhist masters would kill for.

you had a t.v that we put 50 pences
in the back of
we got up late
and concocted dishes bought from the spar,
Your houseplants flourished
and so did your children
we hid in your room
fucking all day
to the occasional sound
of the ice-cream van
then at half three
we got the kids
watched the t.v
then went back to bed
at the time I had aspirations
that's why I went
but those days
with the world outside the glass
of your bedroom window
were the best so far

The Atlantis myth re-ravelled

I'm talking about the allegory of A0 sheets of paper impregnated with flower petals more expensive than a kings Cross crack habit, you can get your cock sucked down there for less than the price of a set of Rotring pens. But we all prefer to kid ourselves with an antiquated value system that only Greek restaurants should maintain, you can see it behind the glass skewered up, ready for the fire but they won't tell you what it is, you can detect aubergine, you can detect green peppers but what's the grey flesh?
Lambporkchickenpig.
Lambporkchickenpig
We live in a vale of testosterone consoled by chicken popcorn that semantically turns into meals when you add coke and chips

Then kids! go out and become Tim Henman.

We're all vulnerable but not all of us can express this, some people are dextrous some are ambidextrous most of us are ambiguous some people know how to put up dexion. Guilding Dutch metal onto hardboard doesn't make you an icon painter
Ecstasy is not that dangerous,
And you're not that special.

Colin Lowe and Roddy Thomson
*Imbition*
2002
Vodka bottles, dispensers and vinyl on linen
200 x 120 cm

# BART WELLS INSTITUTE

## PRESS RELEASE FOR *ANOTHER SHITTY DAY IN PARADISE*

Saturday 21st September to Sunday 3rd November 2002. A group exhibition featuring Phillip Allen, Gianpaolo Cottino, Colin Lowe and Roddy Thomson, Francis Upritchard, Billy Childish and Luke Gottelier.

### PHILLIP ALLEN

"You get the feeling that, in their lifetime, Phillip Allen's paintings have served an alternative purpose. Painted on gessoed board, they appear like grubby, paint-encrusted tabletops flipped on their axis."

*Rebecca Geldard*

"The patterns and shapes he uses undoubtedly betray an interest in cartoon imagery, but this is subsumed within the broader concerns... For the most part Allen keeps his paint thin, brushing and smudging a surface that could be sky, land, and the space of imagination all at once."

*Michael Archer*

### GIANPAOLO COTTINO

Bart Wells Institute is proud to announce its first artist-in-residence. A graduate of the University of Westminster, Gianpaolo Cottino is currently working on-site at the Institute. Born in Zambia in 1972 the artist spent his childhood in Italy, his adolescence in South Africa and moved to England in 1997.

### COLIN LOWE AND RODDY THOMSON

a) what do you want us to do?
b) can we afford to do it.
c) is it worth doing.
d) scratch a b and c, we'll do what we want.

### FRANCIS UPRITCHARD

"I took acid once which was quite bad. Y'know how some people can take 12 acid tabs and still talk to you? I had a terrible experience. I'd taken this acid I wasn't feeling very happy about it so I said to my friend Paul 'I feel bad, take me home'. I was living at home at the time. I'd come home, taken off all my clothes, jumped out the window and run down the street. So Paul chased after me. Kind of dragged me back after a group of guys had got out of the car and said 'What are you doing to this woman?'. He managed to explain it, dragged me back home. I'd been shouting my father's name over and over again in a high pitch scream. My whole family were at home. My little brother said he'd never heard such long held high pitched screaming in his life. So eventually mum came in to find out what was going on. And I, naked, jumped onto her from the floor above, wrestled her to the ground and bit her on the arm. I don't even remember it. In the morning I had bruises all over me. I'd eaten my Venus Fly trap plants."

*Interview with Harry Pye, Log Illustrated, May 2001*

### BILLY CHILDISH

Born in 1959 in Chatham, Kent, Billy Childish left Secondary education at 16 an undiagnosed dyslexic. Refused an interview at the local art school he entered Chatham Naval Dockyard as an apprentice stonemason. During the following six months he produced some six hundred drawings. On the basis of this work he was accepted into St Martin's School of Art. However, his acceptance was short-lived and before completing the course he was expelled for his outspokenness and unorthodox working methods. Childish then spent 12 years "painting on the dole". In a twenty year period he has published 30 collections of his poetry, recorded over 70 full-length independent LP's and produced over 1,000 paintings.

LUKE GOTTELIER is the curator of the exhibition.

### BART WELLS INSTITUTE FILM PROGRAMME

The film programme is an evening of cinema complementary to each exhibition. It is programmed by Mark Aerial Waller from his project *The Wayward Canon*. The film night for *Another Shitty Day in Paradise* will feature *Joe Meek Shall Inherit the Earth* a drama documentary about Britain's first independent record producer and creator of the space rock sound, as represented by a cast of beer cans. For subscribe to the mailing list for the Bart Wells Institute film programme and exhibitions email thebartwells@hotmail.com and for more information on *Wayward Canon Cinema* email waywardcanon@bigfoot.com.

### EXHIBITIONS PROGRAMME

The next exhibition at the Bart Wells Institute will be *Tombs of the Fantasy Undead* curated by Sam Basu.

For further information about *Another Shitty Day in Paradise* telephone 020 7256 0739. Open Saturdays and Sundays 12-6pm.

# THE BART WELLS INSTITUTE ARTIST-IN-RESIDENCE PROGRAMME

# GIANPAOLO COTTINO INTERVIEWED BY SAM BASU

: Last night I was in the pub and I met this guy. He was convinced that the Bart Wells Institute shows were in the 1990s and not in the 21st Century. He really felt it should have come from then. What were you doing then?

GIANPAOLO COTTINO: I had just left film school in Cape Town and was travelling around South Africa and Mozambique.

SB: What was happening there at that time?

GC: It was just after the civil war in 1992 – 93 but nobody was going there, it wasn't a holiday destination, but it was fantastic because you were in a place that had not been opened up and nobody knew what was in there. We hitchhiked, and a scientologist picked us up.

SB: Was it safe?

GC: Maputo was always relatively safe, it's the capital and very southern and only came under direct attack a few times in that whole 20 years. Getting to the city on the long road you take from the South African border was just trucks and cars and tanks and aeroplanes on the side of the road, all blown up. There was a real sense that there had been a war the moment you stepped over the border.

SB: How come you went there?

GC: Well it was still a beautiful place …

SB: … crushed by the war. So when you were artist-in-residence at the Bart Wells, that was almost like a performance. Because you had a building interconnected with a group of people, and a series of exhibitions.

GC: It was not a piece. When Bart Wells was going on I was still thinking about objects, sculptures …

SB: … the more traditional art object. You were making drawings and objects. The piece you showed at the Bart Wells was a sculpture, but it had some wine glasses?

GC: Port.

SB: There was an invitation to be social around the piece.

GC: To be social, but to specifically enter into a dialogue. There were two glasses and it was port, not vodka or … I was looking for something melodic and slow rather than …

SB: getting drunk?

GC: Yeah, that you would sit down and do something slow, and so it was port. And it got drunk.

SB: One of the interesting things that you did on the residency was to build a mirror gallery. But not to set up in competition with the Bart Wells or to form a subgroup.

GC: No.

SB: Was it a model of an artist-run space, a functioning space within another space?

GC: It could have been, but I did not make it like that. I made it as an object. This cube, this gallery, was an object but you could see that I did not make four white walls and a ceiling.

SB: It was not the "professional" space that it mirrored but the artist's solution to the exhibiting space, like the Bart Wells itself, rather than the commercial or institutional art space. And not just because it was a bit crumby and made of old rubbish. It opened it up.

GC: ?

SB: There is something about artist-run art spaces that is different. There are no other criteria like education, society building, or increasing real estate value.

GC: Bart Wells was just totally different. There were other spaces operating with a similar form, finding a building and getting some artists together. But with Bart Wells there was more and the more was that it was serious, there was a strictness about it.

SB: I think that it was something to do with the scale. The Bart Wells was trying to run as an institution, though it never was one except in name. It was an artist-run space, but one notch higher. An artist-run museum. Emulating and by that subverting and undermining what institutions do.

GC: I think that there is a particular quality about Bart Wells and artist-run spaces. Firstly there is the visual element that is different from the big money institutions.

SB: It was a dump.

GC: Yes, you are working within an architecture that is crumbling and just waiting to be changed.

SB: Demolished.

GC: So it is in this place of in-between, a space that is not what it was and isn't what it is going to be. It allows people to tap into their own visions.

SB: It is also necessity that forces artists into these crumbling spaces, but the fact that it works keeps us there.

GC: There are a lot of people working in these kinds of spaces, I have done it myself before, where I have inserted myself into a space like that. It can be very hard, and very difficult to find yourself in a space like that.

SB: Was your memory of being on the residency quite grim?

GC: Yeah, now in retrospect we can talk about it but while the actual living experience was happening I could not be analytical about it. I was just trying to deal with it. It was bizarre. It felt different from what was going on next door in the actual gallery spaces. Suddenly there were all these people, I did not know who they were and at the beginning I was climbing through a window in the street to get into the residency in the morning and coming back out at night.

SB: So the invitation was "If you break in next door you can have the residency."

GC: Someone else was going to take the space but had disappeared so I decided to break into next door because I was in the middle of something and I wanted to stay and see it through.

SB: So you knocked through the wall.

GC: I broke the wall down. But it was raining inside the space and I needed a dry area to leave my drawings in.

SB: These things can only pop up when a building loses its previous use – there is a no man's land. With the Bart Wells there were successive changes from the first show where the pigeon shit was still visible through to the last show. Each show had introduced another white wall or painted something. They even made off with a box of spotlights from the old Saatchi gallery. It was slowly impersonating the institution. It stopped at just the right time. It would have got core funding next.

GC: I remember that even at the time of the shows this was a talking point, whether that was the direction it should be going in, using the language of the institution, like writing about the artist on the walls. I think that in retrospect looking at some of the artists that exhibited it was as if the building went along with them towards bigger things.

SB: A natural progression. But it was heading towards being the institute that it sought to subvert.

GC: So do you develop and what do you develop into? How can you retain this quality long term?

SB: I am not sure if you can, it has to evaporate. You just have to accept it. When it gets neutralised you start on the next project.

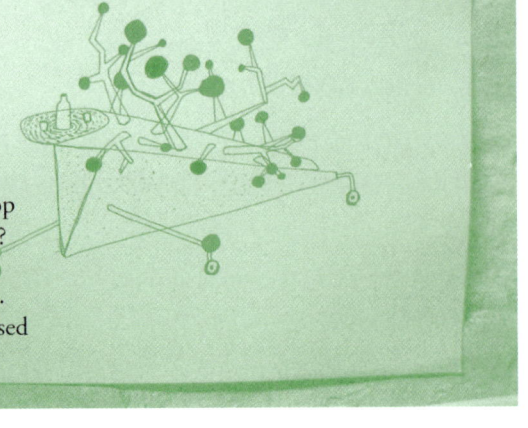

Gianpaolo Cottino
*Place for Exchange*
2002
Mixed media
(detail)

The Bart Wells Institute artist-in-residence studios with works in progress by Gianpaolo Cottino

*Another Shitty Day in Paradise* installation view. *Canopic Urns* by Francis Upritchard and paintings by Luke Gottelier

The sole purchase for the duration of Bart Wells Institute was this urn by Francis Upritchard, which was bought by Rut Blees Luxemburg for €195

*Another Shitty Day in Paradise* installation view with works by Francis Upritchard, Luke Gottelier and Phillip Allen

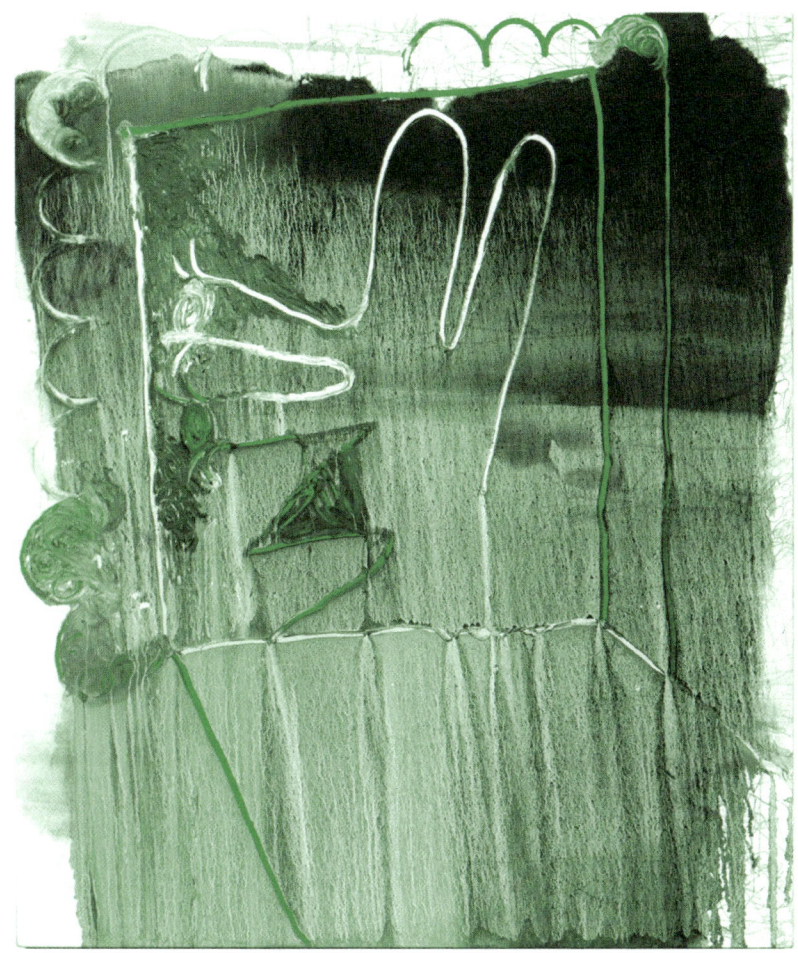

Luke Gottelier
*Rabbit Looking in the Mirror*
2002
Oil on canvas
127 x 107 cm

Phillip Allen
*Achievement and Retention*
2002
Oil on board
112 x 244 cm, diptych in two parts
Courtesy The Approach, London

Luke Gottelier
*Wheelbarrow Man*
2002
Oil on canvas
127 x 112 cm

Phillip Allen
*The Falstrom (Soft Contact Version)*
2002
Oil on board
40 x 50 cm
Courtesy The Approach, London

# THE WAYWARD CANON & THE BART WELLS INSTITUTE FILM PROGRAMME

The Wayward Canon was invited to present films at Bart Wells Institute as well as to become the Institute's cinema programmer, curated to complement the exhibition programme.

The Wayward Canon started out in a disused cab office showing films that were made commercially but had fallen into the margins of cultural importance. These included the pangeneric films of Edgar G. Ulmer, the Art Schlock of Dario Argento, Dennis Hopper's directorial films, and George Franju's post-surrealist, pre-nouvelle vague masterpieces; films which slid on cultural ice and fired in all directions of critical reception. It began with small scale meetings of a quite critical nature. Each one was accompanied by a lengthy introduction, and people actually made notes during screenings. The Wayward Canon continues to run, but no longer in the cab office, as it now engages with durational all night events and cinematic unfoldings for larger audiences.

In the following text are two of the surviving introductions from the Bart Wells Institute film programme.

— Mark Aerial Waller

---

WELCOME TO THE WAYWARD CANON AND PABLO PICASSO!

TONIGHT'S PROGRAMME, SELECTED IN RESPONSE TO THE LIFE AND WORK OF PABLO PICASSO, ELABORATES ON HIS INTEREST IN THE PRIMITIVE BEAST WRITHING AT THE HEART OF MODERNITY AND THE EMERGENCE OF ANALYTIC CUBISM. PICASSO'S WORK EXTENDED FROM THE POETRY OF APOLLINAIRE, WHERE THE CONSCIOUS, DELIBERATE DISSOCIATION AND RECOMBINATION OF ELEMENTS INTO A NEW ARTISTIC ENTITY WAS MADE SELF-SUFFICIENT BY ITS RIGOROUS ARCHITECTURE. HERE TONIGHT WE FOLLOW THESE THOUGHTS WITH TWO FILMS AND AN ENTR'ACTE. THE FIRST FILM IS GEORGES FRANJU'S **Le Sang des Bêtes**, MADE IN 1948. FRANJU, WHO COFOUNDED LA CINÉMATHEQUE FRANÇAIS, MADE FILMS AS RITUAL MACHINES TO BRING THE WORK OF HIS HEROES BACK FROM THE GRAVE. TONIGHT'S HERO IS ELI LOTAR, THE SURREALIST PHOTOGRAPHER WHOSE WORK FEATURED PROMINENTLY IN BATAILLE'S DOCUMENT PUBLICATIONS. THIS FILM, LIKE LOTAR'S PHOTOGRAPHS, IS NOT AN EXPRESSION OF CONCERN FOR THE ANIMALS SLAUGHTERED IN THE MEAT FACTORY, BUT AN OBJECTIVE ACCOUNT OF THE ASTONISHING AMOUNT OF BLOOD ON WHICH CHRISTENDOM SUSTAINS ITSELF DAILY. BATAILLE WRITES, 'THE SLAUGHTERHOUSE IS CURSED AND QUARANTINED LIKE A PLAGUE-RIDDEN SHIP. GOOD FOLK ARE LED TO vegetate as far from the slaughterhouse as possible, to exile themselves out of propriety to a flabby world in which nothing fearful remains and in which to the ineradicable obsession of shame, they are reduced to eating cheese.'

So Franju has two main quests with this film, one is to re-present Eli Lotar's work within the medium of film, to bring the lover's kiss in close proximity to the slaughterman's blade. The other is to bring death into life, to resurrect – the beasts continue trying to gallop back to the land of the living even after the act of killing. His film **Le Sang des Bêtes** continuously holds the beasts back from death with every screening, just as it will do for us tonight.

Following this there will be an entr'acte by Peter Cook and Dudley Moore called **Back of the Cab**. Treat yourselves to drinks and Luke Gottelier's fresh ice creams...

Now we move to **Scarlet Street**, Fritz Lang's bitter critique on the underhand economics encountered by a Sunday painter when he brushes up against the wrong sort of girl.

Have a great evening!"

Peter Cook and Dudley Moore as Derek and Clive

Stills from *Le Sang des Bêtes*, Georges Franju (1949)

| Rat Life and Diet in North America (1968) 16m | Mark Aerial Waller's Wayward Canon Cinema PRESENTS | Billy Jack (1971) 115m |
|---|---|---|
|  A family of draft dodging rats escape upstream to Canada |  ANOTHER SHITTY DAY IN PARADISE FILM NIGHT SUNDAY 20TH NOVERMBER 5PM BART WELLS INSTITUTE  3 Silesia Buildings, London E8  020 7256 0739  thebartwells@hotmail.com homemade ice cream and fresh popcorn available |  "Where there is power, there can never be love, and where there is love, there is no need for power." |

## WELCOME TO THE WAYWARD CANON AND ANOTHER SHITTY DAY IN PARADISE!

Tonight's two films celebrate hope and idealism in North American radical politics. **Rat Life and Diet** (14 mins) was made by Joyce Wieland in 1968 as a protest film and celebration of her native country, Canada. The American people are plagued by cute rodents which escape an urban penitentiary for the rural ideal of Wieland's homeland. At that time Canada was opening its doors to American draft dodgers. Jonas Mekas writes in 1969 in a catalogue for the screening at Museum of Art, Carnegie Institute:

> "It may be about the best (or richest) political movie around. It's all about rebels (enacted by real rats) and police (enacted by real cats). After a long suffering under the cats, the rats break out of prison (in full scale rebellion) and escape to Canada. There they take up organic gardening with no DDT in the grass. It is a parable, a satire, an adventure movie, or you can call it pop art or any art you want. I find it one of the most original films made recently."¹

1 Mekas wrongly identifies the rodents as rats, they are in fact gerbils.

The Feature tonight, **Billy Jack**, was made in 1970 and became the biggest grossing film of 1973 and the 18th largest grossing picture of all time.

**Billy Jack** illustrates the American radical ideals of the early 1970s which were not just acts of protest, but active means for people to set up projects like the New York Vegetable Allotment Groups who battled against town planners for urban gardens, or the Anthology film Archives and the filmmaker's Coop or in the case of **Billy Jack** the Freedom School, a school for socially discarded children. The film takes place on the edge of town out where the Indian reservation meets the Nixon aligned townspeople. The Director and Actor Tom Laughlin and his producer/actress wife Delores Taylor, made a film which was backed for distribution by Warner Bros in 1971, only to be

Still from *Billy Jack*, Tom Laughlin (1971)

dumped into the B movie porn cinema circuit. The director and producer were incensed by this and blackmailed the studio to let them manage the release themselves. So in 1973 they hired cinemas in a process called Four Walling, where they rented the space themselves and took the profits. The cinemas were manned by personally installed retired Mormons who could be trusted not to steal the takings...

Please enjoy the corn popped by Francis Upritchard.

Still from *Rat Life and Diet in North America*, Joyce Wieland (1968)

Phillip Allen
*Beezerspline (Light Version)*
2002
Oil on board
122 x 152 cm

*Leydenjar (Dark Version)*
2002
Oil on board
41 x 51 cm

Courtesy The Approach, London

I ENCLOSE

FOR

ONE YEAR'S SUBSCRIPTION TO:

NAME ~~NDSN~~ ..........................................

ADDRESS ..........................................

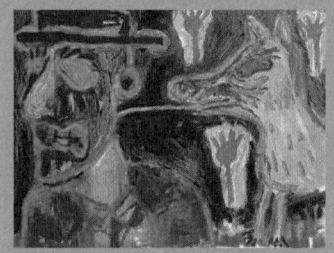

Billy Childish
*Necklicker*
1991
Oil on canvas
38 x 50 cm

*Two Dogs*
1991
Oil on canvas
50 x 38 cm

# TOMBS OF THE UNDEAD FANTACY INSTITUTE

November - December 2002

#7

T.O.F.U.

Caroline Warde

Emma Holmes

Cedar Lewisohn

Goshka Macuga

Sam Basu

Private View Friday 15th November 7-10pm
Saturday 16th November - Sunday 22nd December 2002

Curated by Sam Basu

**BART WELLS INSTITUTE**

3 Silesia Buildings, London E8
07951 454 650 or 07951 746 283

thebartwells@hotmail.com

Open Saturdays and Sundays 12-6pm

# BART WELLS INSTITUTE

3 Silesia Buildings

PRESS RELEASE FOR *TOMBS OF THE FANTASY UNDERDEAD*

*Everything that happened is surrounded by the sense it didn't happen, and these ways of thinking seeping out. Just at one moment there's no such thing as pure evil, and then the next thing you find...*

– The Psykick Boxer

Saturday 16th November – Sunday 22nd December, is a new group exhibition featuring Emma Holmes, Goshka Macuga, Caroline Warde, Sam Basu and Cedar Lewisohn.

## EMMA HOLMES

Emma Holmes' paintings reconnect the architectural into the wallpaper of the psyche; the spaces can no longer continue the monologue of their own failing strategies, and are absorbed into the vocabulary of those who inhabit them. She has escaped the tyranny of the built space and sees them with a gaze that is impervious to modernist allure.

## GOSHKA MACUGA

Macuga has worked by creating collections of paintings or objects within galleries. Different histories, imagined perhaps, but latent and present around the real gallery. Her submission is the very process her work is being placed under in exhibition.

## CAROLINE WARDE

Caroline Warde's leatherette sculptures deftly shift myths. A decapitated head looms out through the history of legend, an omen of castration and catastrophe. But here she has placed it as if it never had a body. The Genesis tale of the seduction of Adam and Eve is reallocated. Here desire arises not from the serpent but from the fruit itself.

## SAM BASU

Basu's drawings inhabit the world of the psychic visionary, and those receiving messages from outer space. By immersing himself in examples of 'inspired' behaviour he hopes to divine what making art might be. His first big clue came whilst watching "Close Encounters of the Third Kind".

## CEDAR LEWISOHN

Lewisohn's paintings are constructed of the bland, manufactured, disposables of urban life. His motivation to paint does not seem to come from art history. He is always on the side, but he is filling the space he has found himself in the grit and beauty of what he finds out there. He is our new war reporter; transforming our attempts at escape into the materials of our estrangement.

SAM BASU is the curator of the exhibition.

## BART WELLS INSETITUTE FILM PROGRAMME

The Bart Wells Institute opening night for *Tombs of the Fantasy Underdead* will be a screening of *Nosferatu* introduced and performed with a newly commissioned soundtrack live by Tabar... Further live music to be confirmed, with DJs by The Cock Rockers. To subscribe to the mailing list for the Bart Wells Institute film programme and exhibitions email thebartwells@hotmail.com.

## EXHIBITIONS PROGRAMME

The next exhibition at the Bart Wells Institute will be *International Tourist*, curated by David Thorpe.

For further information about *Tombs of the Fantasy Underdead* telephone 020 8855 4164. Open Saturdays and Sundays 12–6

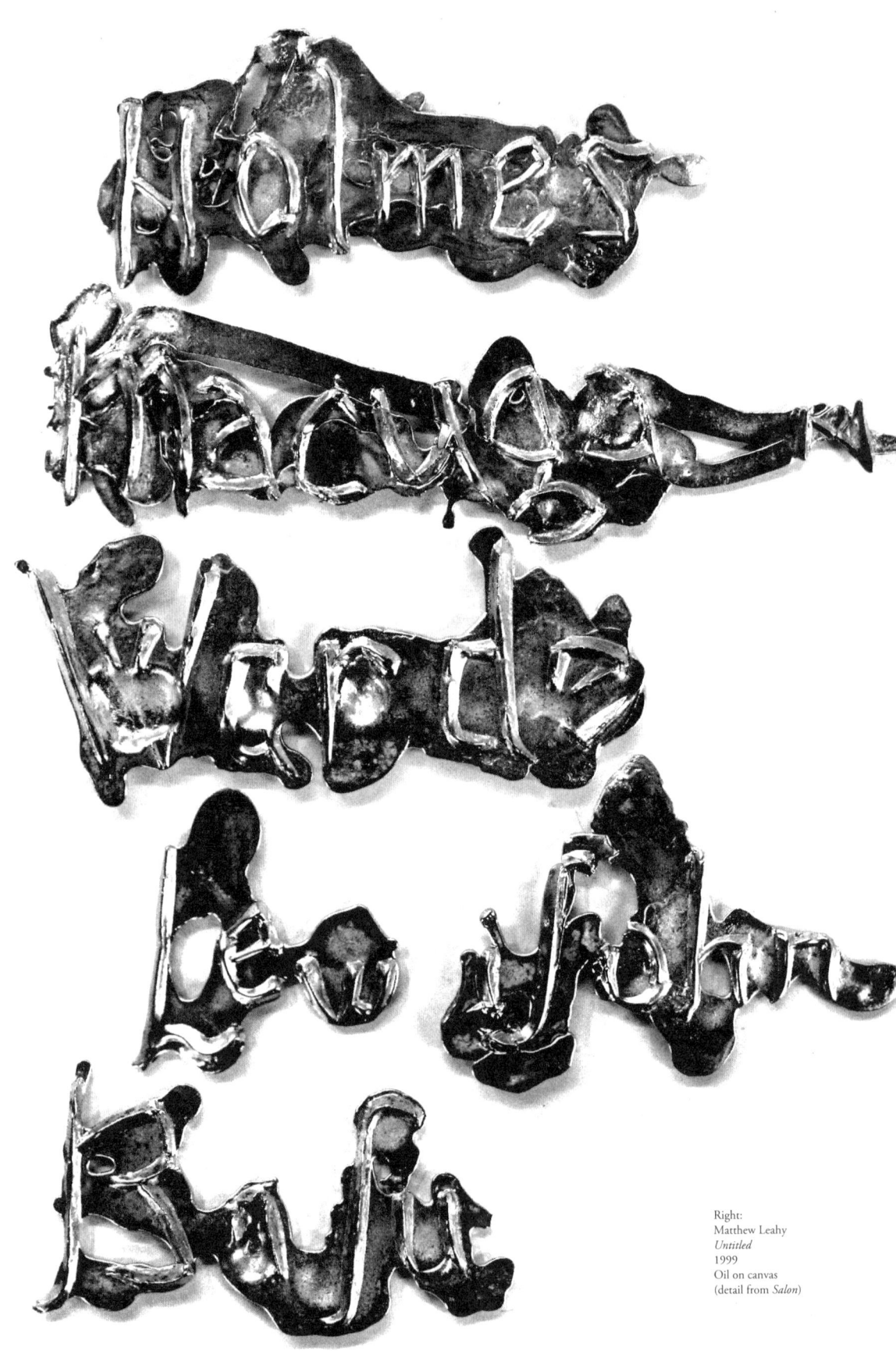

Right:
Matthew Leahy
*Untitled*
1999
Oil on canvas
(detail from *Salon*)

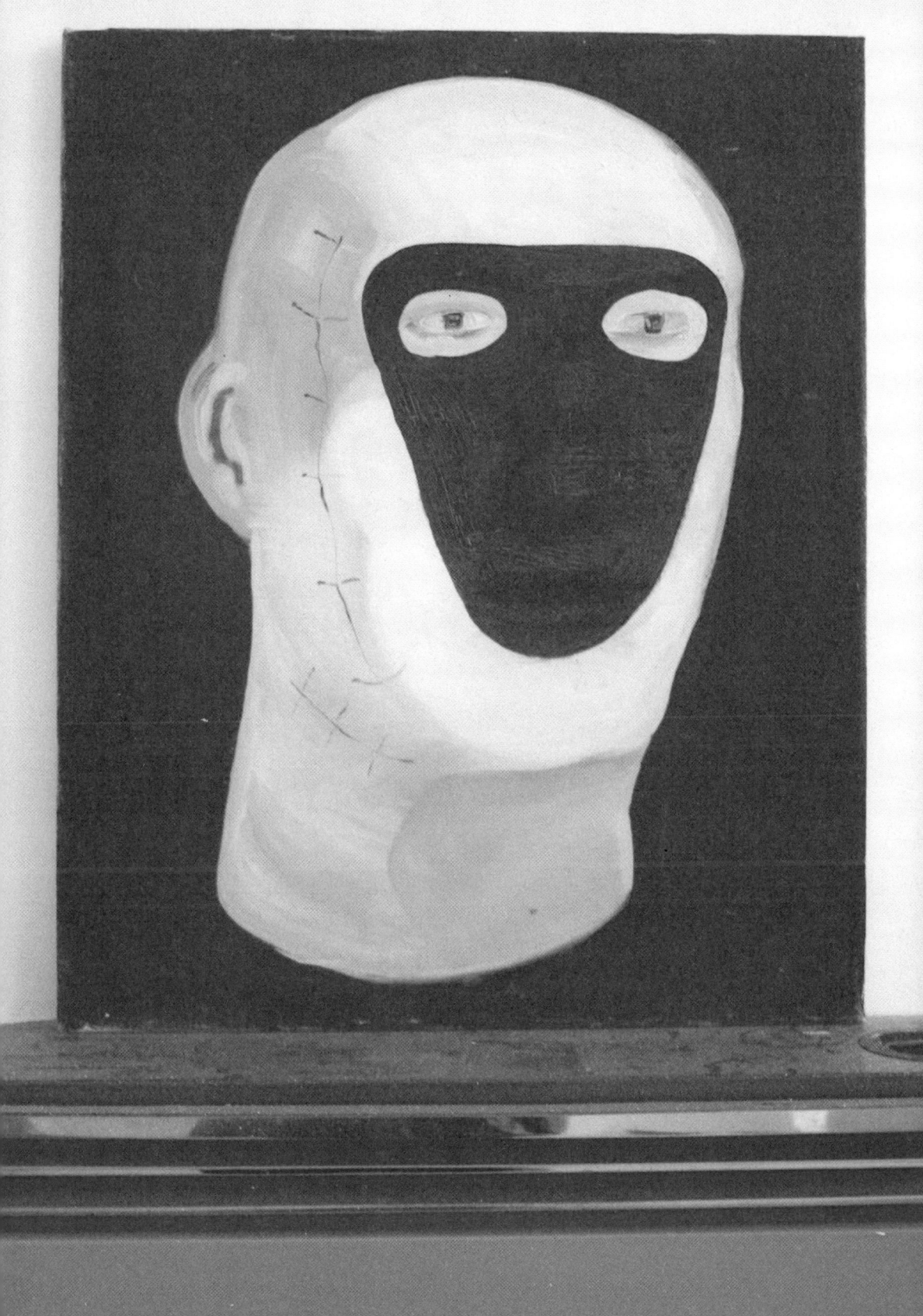

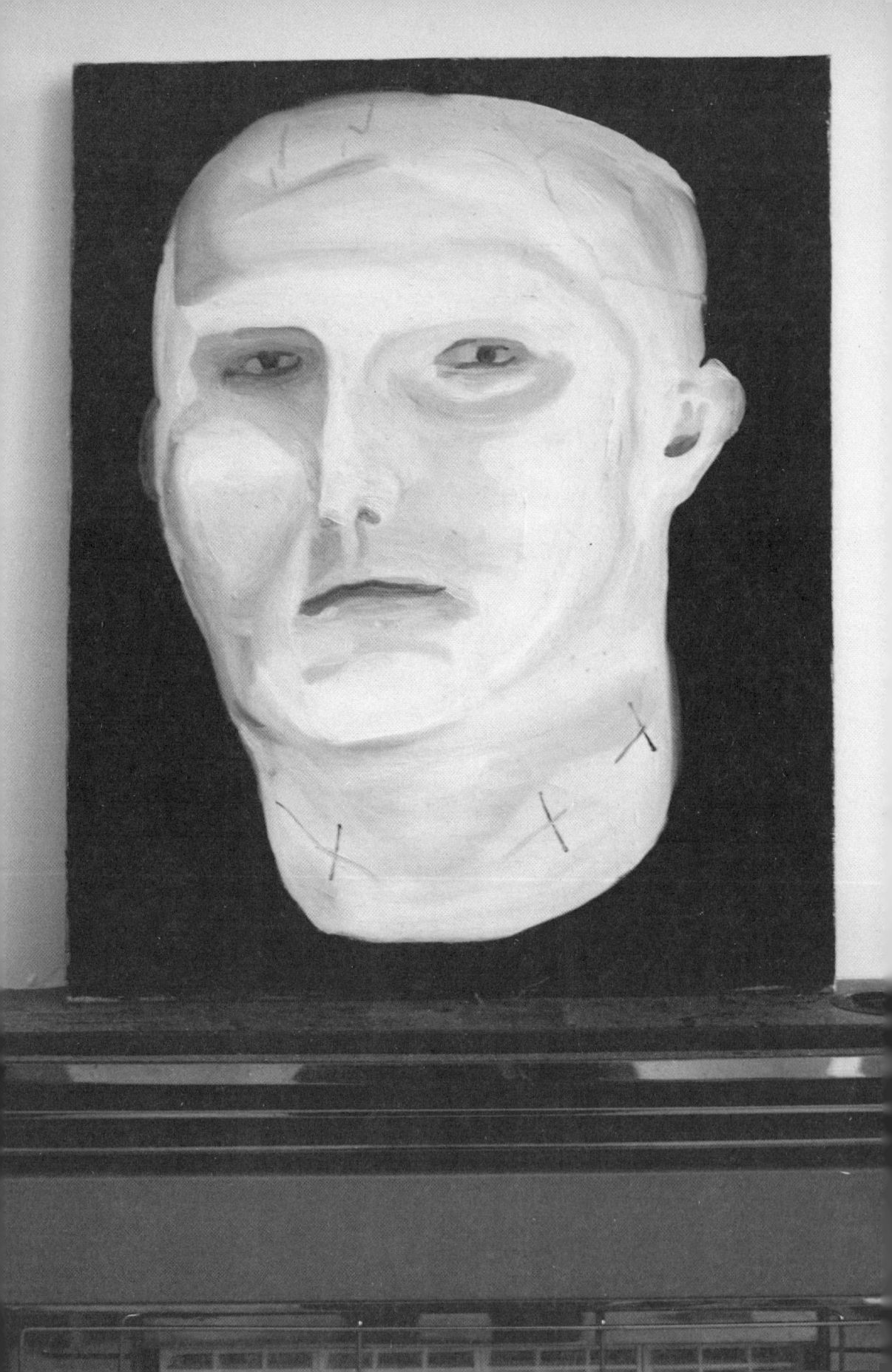

Next double spread:
Goshka Macuga
*Salon*
2002
Mixed media
Dimensions variable
Courtesy Kate MacGarry, London

Sabina Chojecka
*Oboz Jencow Radzieckich w Ostrowku Wegrowskim. Roku 1941-42*
67 x 67 cm
(detail from *Salon*)

Left:
Matthew Leahy
*Untitled*
1999
Oil on canvas
(detail from *Salon*)

Cedar Lewisohn
*Drawing from the Play The Mikado (Savoy Theatre)*
2002
Pen and mixed media on paper
21 × 29.7 cm

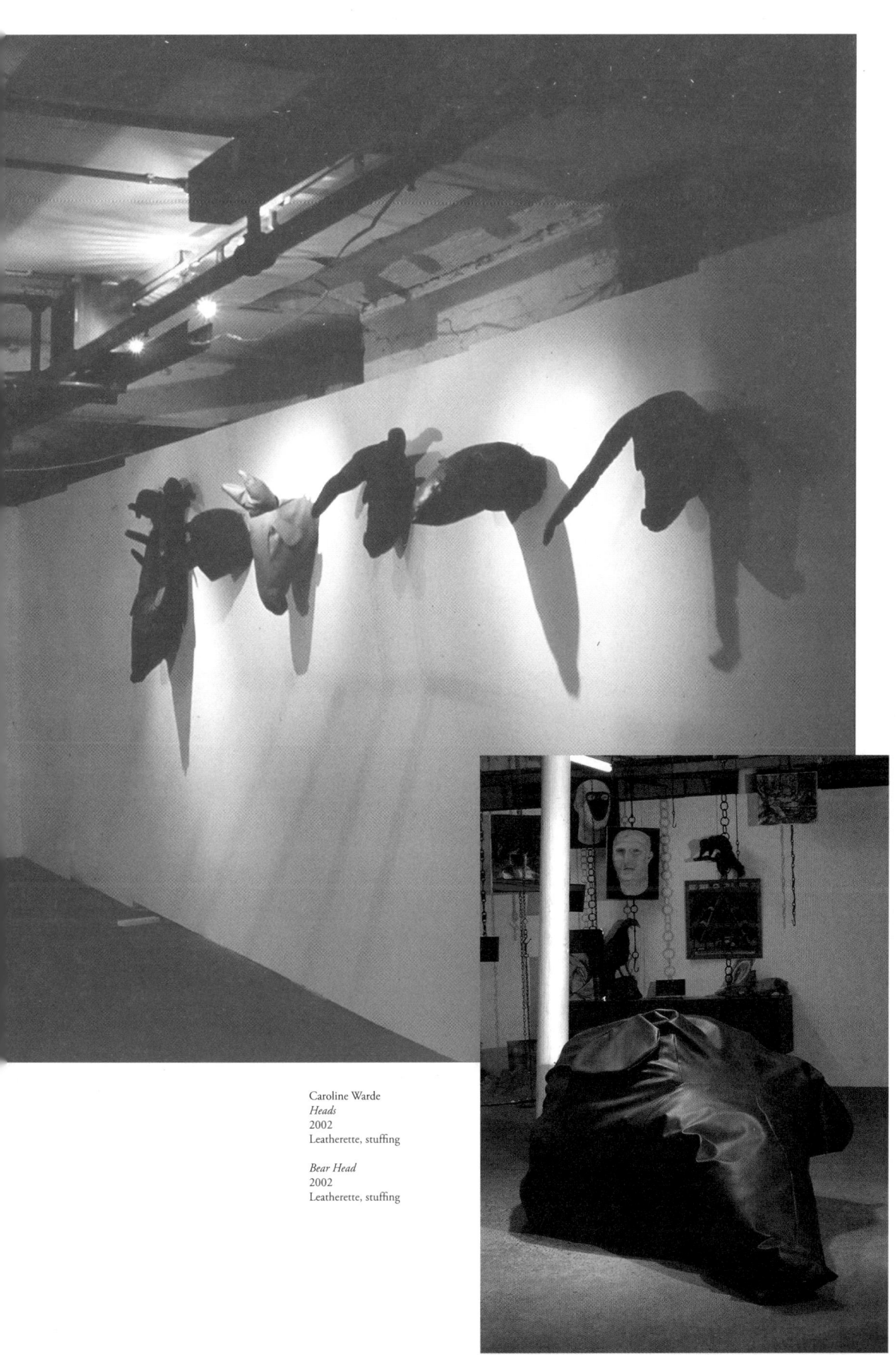

Caroline Warde
*Heads*
2002
Leatherette, stuffing

*Bear Head*
2002
Leatherette, stuffing

Sam Basu
*Transmitted Architecture*
2002
Oil on paper
Dimensions variable

Emma Holmes
*Dentist Appointment, 6pm*
2002
Oil on canvas
127 x 102 cm

**BART WELLS INSTITUTE** AND *TOMBS OF THE FANTASANTASY UNDEAD*

## CHRISTMAS PARTY

LIVE MUSIC BY

### GHOST CLUB

### GO FERAL

### PETCAR

### ART SCHOOL GRADUATE

### NORWEGIAN LADY

Friday 13th December 7.30pm till late
3 Silesia Buildings, London E8
07951 746 283.

# NOSFERATU

### DIRECTED BY F.W. MURNAU 192[?]

### WITH A NEW SOUND-TRACK
### COMPOSED & PERFORMED BY

## PETCAR[D]

FRIDAY 13 DECEMBER 2002, 7.30 PM
ADMISSION FREE
BARTWELLS INSTITUTE
[?] SILESIA BUILDINGS
LONDON E8

*ADMISSION FREE*

# THE FRAGILE UNDERGROUND

## BART WELLS INSTITUTE
### PERIODICAL

# #8

Curated by David Thorpe

Private View Friday 31st January 7-10pm

Saturday 1st February - Sunday 9th March 2003

**BART WELLS INSTITUTE**

3 Silesia Buildings, London E8

Open Saturdays and Sundays 12-6pm     07973 781 523     thebartwells@hotmail.com

# AN UNWILLING CURATOR

## DAVID THORPE INTERVIEWED BY BRUCE HAINES

: How did *The Fragile Underground* begin?

DAVID THORPE: The show didn't really represent any of my tastes a great deal. Eva Berendes was a given as she was helping me at the time. And then I saw Daria Martin and they both had this kind of low-fi, modernist vibe. I knew Scott Myles and Hayley Tompkins and they kind of fitted. I knew Ulli Knall's work, and I put them together like some kind of interior design project. I knew Daria's work was good but no one knew her yet in London. And no one in London knew Scott and Hayley either although their work was shown in Scotland. Ulli was kind of good I thought, but she was ignored because she was making ceramics. It was extremely odd when I was hanging the show that there was hostility about her work. Apart from Scott and Hayley, no one wanted to show their work anywhere near hers, even though I said she went to Goldsmiths and she's not this naïve artist, she knows what she's doing.

BH: Do you know what Ulli is doing now?

DT: No, she started a family but I think she is back doing shows again. No one was supporting her art. My friendship with Eva has never recovered after that show ... nor with Florian; I couldn't bear doing it as a job.

BH: Do you think that one thing that comes out of making an exhibition is that often you start off wanting to work with someone because you like them as a person. Do you think that it is inevitable it ends up changing a relationship?

DT: Initially it was called *The Exhausted Underground* and the artists all said "If it's called that, we all go." And I was like "What the fuck have I done?" I don't even want to do this stupid show. So it was called *The Fragile Underground* instead. Ulli was never there because she had a job and so just gave the work and said to look after it. Scott and Hayley were the most experienced in terms of showing so they were also the most professional in terms of how to discuss the show.

BH: So they were the most flexible?

DT: Yes they were the most flexible. For everyone else it was "their chance" kind of thing. It was extremely awkward and I ended up hating them all. But we can't really talk about that. I was interested in Florian because his work plays on architecture. Initially he said he would build a wall that would encase the cinema. Then he turned up and said "I am not going to build walls for the cinema." But that was the only reason I asked him in there. I didn't just want the stupid wall but I wanted that as an artwork. I thought that was a nice way of integrating any changes in the architectural space. So he said "No I will instead decorate and play on these pillars." So I said "OK." But as I said, his work is almost invisible, like architecture ... and then I put Ulli's work near his and he said "I don't want any work near my work." So I said "Hang on, it's a group show and you said you wanted this work to function like architecture and actually you don't, you want to treat it like sculpture so that you have this flow around it so that you can kind of sit around it and contemplate it." There was a contradiction as to how he wanted the work to be presented. It's kind of invisible but actually it is not. And then at the end when I hung the show he said "You know it would have been kind of a good idea if her work was next to mine" – and you're like "Fuck this!"

BH: Was the building and the fact that it was a squat a hindrance or a help?

DT: It was fine. It was awkward in terms of just how cold it was. I don't think that anyone missed being

in a beautiful space. It might have made certain artists nervous, but for me there was not a problem.
BH: I remember the steep stairs, it was getting forever steeper. And particularly Eva's lights, the curtains, the kind of dinginess really profited from that space, profited that work. And Daria's work was exquisite because it was so carefully orchestrated, yet was presented in this rough context.

DT: We put in all that. I mean I bought the Hessian curtains and the shutterboard to build the chairs that everyone sat on. So you had sort of guerrilla chic in that squat culture. The whole squat culture, even by Bart Wells time, was no longer radical in its gesture as City Racing was. I am sure the artists that lived there – well I can't believe they didn't have money.

BH: But at the same time I think it did lend it a sort of exoticism from the rest of the kind of institutional world going around.

DT: Yes, but the Bart Wells Institute, similar to when I was invigilating City Racing, still was, uhm, no one came. I used to invigilate City Racing. Sometimes you would get three people ... but because it's become this historicised, almost institution, you assume that everyday there were hundreds of people turning up. It was a good day if you had thirteen people coming. And when we were invigilating the Bart Wells show I am not sure if we got more than ten a day. With City Racing I used to add people's names in the book so that it looked as though more people came, just for something to do.

BH: Did you have a show at City Racing?

DT: That was my first show, my debut.

BH: Did you think that the nature of City Racing influenced what you did?

Eva Berendes
*Untitled*
2003
Cotton, fabric dye
380 x 700 cm

*Untitled*
2003
Plastics, electrics
Dimensions variable

DT: I think the spirit of City Racing has influenced most of my thinking within the art world. I think that even though she has become far more successful now than when City Racing was happening, Maureen Paley has remained more separate, her attitude stemmed from the same environment and it showed in her selection of artists ... still against the West End galleries, even though Paul Noble shows with Gagosian etc. as with City Racing there was always this kind of community. If I had gone with one of those blue chip galleries, my general philosophy of life would be different. So even though I have done OK, it is still not about money or the desire to show in a big gallery in order to get a sportscar. I have no interest in showing in the West End galleries. I am happy with Maureen, the 303 kind of ex-hippies who set up on their own without money. Meyer Riegger also set up on similar lines. I feel far more comfortable in that kind of family environment. I think that way of working, and wanting to be around others who also work like that, came from my first experience of working at City Racing.

BH: Were you thinking about that when you did the show at Bart Wells?

DT: Eva's work was interesting - this was a time where she had just graduated, one or two galleries had been sniffing around, but I think they have all folded now – wide boy galleries – there was one gallery that offered her a show and then pulled out and she was very upset. So she needed that first kind of boost, a kind of support. It was good that this show came at a time to be able to do that.

BH: There are not many artists who are that generous about emerging artists' work. Have you always advocated that attitude?

DT: Yes, but I didn't put my name on *The Fragile Underground* either. I think that nowhere was it written "curated by David Thorpe." It was awkward because there is this curator David Thorp and

Daria Martin
*Birds*
2001
16mm film
Courtesy Maureen Paley,
London

he continually gets phone calls saying initially "I didn't know you were making work as well" or whatever and I didn't want to drive him any more insane. And I didn't do it to further any of my own interests.

BH: Do you think artists are better than curators at spotting emerging talent?

DT: I think they might see it in a different way because you are introduced to them on a far more sociable level than a curator. If you say "This is a curator, this is an artist" there is already a kind of business convention going on. Between artists there isn't that. Curators maybe want an official visit, or they go to the final shows. It's fairly arbitrary. There's less nervousness from other artists about showing the work, less expectation. There was only one show I was ever going to curate. It was the only time I would do something myself. Also if I was asked to curate a show now, there aren't five or six artists I could immediately think of putting in.

BH: So you don't have a kind of dream line-up for an exhibition now?

DT: There is, but they are all long dead.

BH: What do you remember most about the show?

DT: The thing I remember most was the awkwardness of being a curator for the first time. Before, I was always in group shows where you work with curators. Often as an artist, doing a group show, you do it because you trust the curator, and you give the work over. In this case, because I knew everyone far more closely, there wasn't that distance. There was far more discussion, argument and

Daria Martin
*Birds*
2001
16mm film
Courtesy Maureen Paley, London

debate about where things should go. So I had to adopt a different role and I didn't enjoy it. I found that difficult. I found artists incredibly egocentric, and as an artist I obviously am too, but then as a curator I found that extremely frustrating.

BH: Being a curator is like being a priest or vicar, you have to be this pastoral figure. But lots of curators have egos that can get in the way too.

DT: Yeah, but also in the Bart Wells thing there was no support structure there. Essentially Luke asked if I wanted to do a show, but most of it I had to fund by myself. I think they got the drinks in, possibly. So you had to do things slowly, had to organise far more stuff than you wanted to. I think someone like Daria, for instance, didn't know the London arts scene and thought there would be far more support than there was.

BH: Was that the most difficult thing for you, realising you had this responsibility?

DT: Yeah, I thought just pick four or five artists, but then you had to organise transportation, work out the administration. It was difficult, essentially an unpleasant experience.

BH: Luke said that Bart Wells was about the artist as curator. That was why he wanted to do it. He

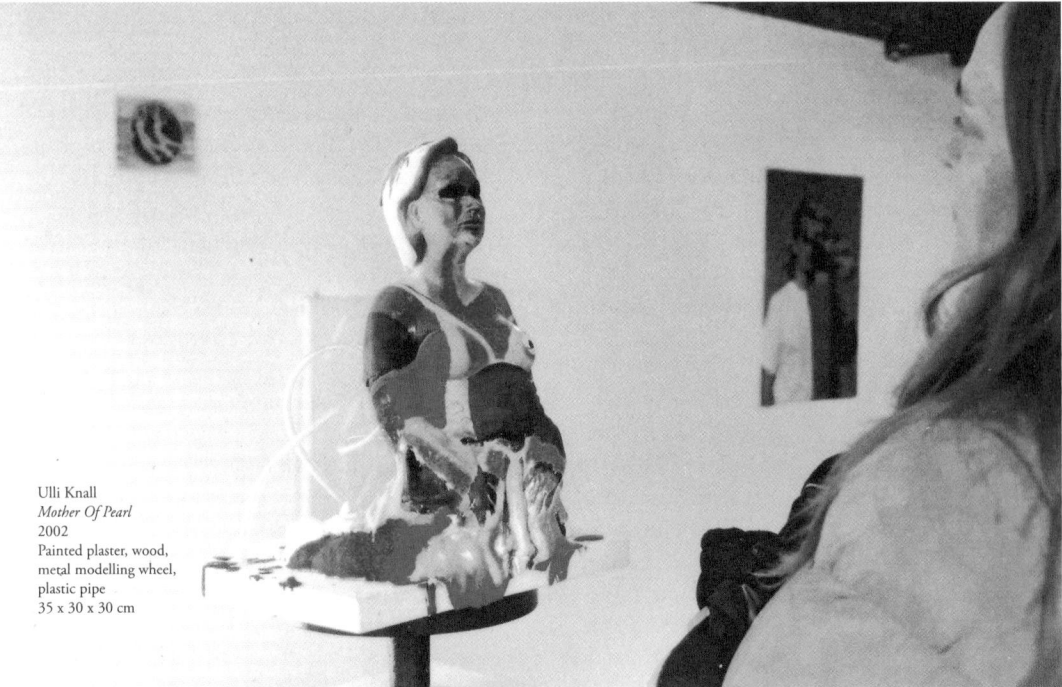

Ulli Knall
*Mother Of Pearl*
2002
Painted plaster, wood, metal modelling wheel, plastic pipe
35 x 30 x 30 cm

can't have meant the artist as administrator. He didn't want to give you a hard time either.

DT: No, but if I ask someone to participate, then I feel I have to take some responsibility. I get extremely annoyed when I talk to younger artists and they say that this person has given me a show then it turns out they have to pay their own transportation and crates. I think that's extremely one-sided. It still happens to me. So I had to take on board this element of organisation, and within the budget I had to provide as much as I could.

BH: Would you do it again?

DT: I would be very nervous. I would do it again if circumstances were the same, as Luke and that were close friends, it's not like a professional approach, you say yeah, and it's while you are in a bar or club. Once you agree you have to do it. But I have no desire to do it.

BH: But you were involved in a show before with Brian Griffiths, you must have known in some way what to expect?

DT: Me and Brian showed a film we had already made (cf. p. 37), but I didn't have any role in terms of organisation. I did the bar downstairs, selling the drinks with Eva.

BH: Did he express to you any anxieties about having to look after the needs of artists? Did he have as much of a hard time at Bart Wells as you did?

DT: He struggled to remember. I think he was OK, he just went around and picked up the work and largely organised it himself. My problem was that in part I was unsure of myself as a curator, an unwilling curator. As an artist I wouldn't necessarily want to be interfered with, so I didn't want to do that either.

BH: Do you think curators have a responsibility to interrogate an artist's practice?

DT: I never thought I was a curator, I never asked for new work; there were particular pieces I wanted. I knew what I was getting. I knew Scott's piece; what Hayley would show; I had already seen Daria's piece; so then there was no need for discussion afterwards. I would never begin to ask questions about the works, you kind of accept the works or not. It wasn't some kind of testament.

Florian Balze
*Offenbach*
2003
Texture paint with sand, strips of brass on plasterboard
255 x 32 x 32 cm/255 x 32 x 15 cm

BH: Did you accept responsibility for how they would be seen, as most hadn't shown in London before? Were you nervous for them or were they nervous themselves?

DT: Although it was the first time I think she had shown in London, Daria had already done things in L.A. She is extremely strong in terms of how she wants her work portrayed. The main thing was that she needed a cinema space upstairs, and we talked about the aesthetics of how that might look, and once that was done it was quite straightforward. Scott and Hayley had done as many shows as I had, so I didn't want or need to tell them anything.

BH: What was the best thing that happened in the show?

DT: The best thing is that they all got interest, I think, or most of them did. I think with Daria I was just lucky to be the person who was at Delfina with her to say "OK, I am doing a show" and the next day she showed me her work, and it's so good I was able to just build the show around it. If I hadn't shown it, two days later someone else would have seen it and thought "My God, this is wonderful" and

shown it elsewhere. Eva did well out of it. As I said earlier, there's always a myth that these places were more popular than they were, but the people that came could move some of the artists onto another stage very quickly. I think Kate MacGarry saw new artists there; Darren Flook I think showed Scott and Hayley very soon afterwards; Maureen Paley is now working with Daria.

BH: Do you think artist-curated shows acknowledge the influence artists have on curators anyway, in the way curators, such as myself, are always asking other artists who they like?

DT: I think artists, curators and gallerists' backgrounds are so slippery; certain curators were artists; they haven't studied curating, they studied art, others art history. A lot of gallerists are ex-artists. It's only recently you have these professional curators coming out of the likes of the Royal College. I think beforehand it was always a fluid thing. I imagine someone like Jake Miller or Maureen as an artist; initially there's a crossover and that when they set up their spaces they're doing their own work. You don't always think when you set up that it's going to end up in ten years time opening a huge space in the West End. I think artist-curated shows are less likely to thematise a grand claim or statement. Some curators seem to want to use group shows for this grand theme, and the work is kind of fitted in. Artists won't make such a bold angle on it.

BH: It's funny, other curators think it's lazy not to have that strong argument around a show.

DT: But the theme becomes extremely arbitrary. It allows weak work to be included to promote an idea when the most important thing is to get a collection of strong work.

BH: Is there anything about the Bart Wells show that reflected upon your own practice or your own interests?

DT: Do you think there were any similarities? It felt different, but then I am thinking about how I divided spaces up; the cinema, Eva's screens, maybe in terms of how I was using screens in my installations. It was about the same time as ... how long ago was the show?

BH: It must have been six years ago.

DT: It was as I was developing from making pure collages to making paintings and objects, seeing how you arrange a show, almost like readymades in part, seeing how certain objects and divisions of spaces could work together. It gave me encouragement in the way I wanted to go in my own work. The shows I made shortly after for Art Now at the Tate and Meyer Riegger also had that feeling

of almost being a group show. The watercolours, collages and screens could have a relationship but also be in different styles. I stopped talking about these ideal communities but somehow you could get a community of objects. The work doesn't have to share the same kind of aesthetic or use of the hand, but they blend into one another, like works in a tightly curated show. This show helped my thinking of how that would work.

BH: Did you write the press release?

DT: Me and Brian did the press release when we were both quite tipsy; it feels dated now, but there was this low-fi modernist aesthetic, a lot in Glasgow, a lot in London, and it probably still is going around. We wanted the press release to have the same casualness.

BH: It anticipated the Tate Triennial in some ways two or three years later; you were not so much defining what was going on at the time but anticipating perhaps what would be going on in the future?

DT: I forgot Tommy Støckel was in it as well. I was teaching a little bit at Goldsmiths and gave tutorials

Ulli Knall
*Morning Glory*
2002
Painted ceramics and gesmonite
160 x 40 x 40 cm

Scott Myles
*Untitled (Nothing)*
2002
Pencil on paper
Three framed drawings each 55 x 70 cm
Courtesy The Modern Institute/Toby Webster Ltd., Glasgow

to Florian. So you knew there were certain things that were going on, just that it hadn't been shown publicly at that stage in London. A lot of galleries hadn't seen the work as these people were still studying, were friends of friends, or were helping me or others and they knew each other socially.

BH: What did Tommy do?

DT: Tommy showed one photograph of himself becoming this abstract cube thing, I think.
BH: "A man consumed by his passion for the Modernist architecture that surrounds him ..."

DT: If I did it again I would never make a press release like that again, it's become such a cliché. If I were to do something now it would be far harder.

BH: But at that time it was unusual to have such a succinct sentence about the artist.

DT: The first thing you do when you go into art spaces is look at the press release, and then collapse into fits of laughter, because there's an attempt at a kind of pseudo philosophy written by someone with no sense of grammar and an absurd quality of writing. We wanted this simple, dumb, quite playful text.

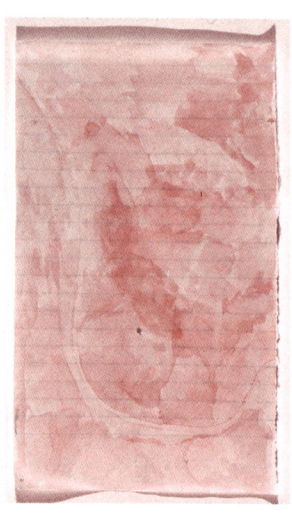 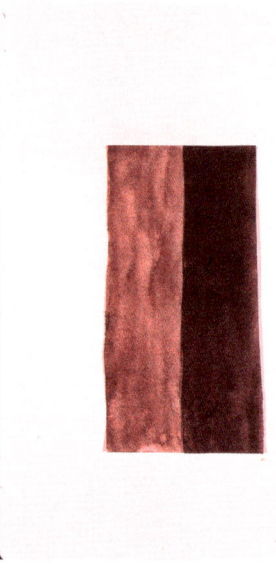 

BH: The spirit of the press release is the spirit in which your own work is read too. When you reflect on something that took place five or six years ago it's rather like reflecting on an old relationship, you tend to only remember the good bits.

DT: That's what's strange about it. I think it did have an influence on me as well, because I think the work I was making at the time wouldn't have fitted into that show, but the work I was making after at *The Colonists* show at Art Now would have fitted in. One reason for curating a show is also to put in artists you are kind of jealous of. There are elements and certain freedoms of Scott's practice I am envious of as an artist, where he has a kind of, I wouldn't say a casualness, but there's a …

BH: A slacker quality?

DT: Where I am spending 20 hours in a studio, he can fabricate something, come up with a gesture.

BH: He isn't bound to a craft.

DT: I am philosophically bound up with the craft element to impart certain ideas I have about the work.

BH: While you acknowledge the labour you put into the work, it isn't the overriding memory of your experience of it.

DT: *I am Golden*, the indoor garden I made in 2002 had a kind of Americana wilderness, pioneer quality to it. That made me nervous I was adopting a kind of hillbilly chic. From that I wanted to see where it came from, that do-it-yourself, homemadeness, survivalist aesthetic. I thought I could make a link to the Arts and Crafts movement, which threw me back to a kind of English, William Morris, Ruskin kind of tradition.

BH: What was particularly unique about what Bart Wells Institute was doing that doesn't exist now?

DT: Most artists have a generation of friends. It can be done again; I think it was done beforehand. I think what was kind of curious about it was that both me, Brian, Luke, we just took it as that was the space we had. The fact it was a squat no longer had any kind of resonance. While there was no budget as such, there was no sense of doing squat art. The fragile underground, not necessarily the exhausted underground; there was this sense of art being linked to squat shows being a counter to the mainstream gallery culture. But we already knew that was nonsense. Saatchi came around and so on. The idea that something has more worth because it is in a rough space I no longer believe in. So many artists that came out of the Eighties or early Nineties moved into the commercial world and set up these galleries. Now you see younger spaces open up straight away as commercial spaces. City Racing I think only ever sold one piece of art. They really were not interested. By 1995–96 the world had changed quite a bit within the art world. Often people put on squat shows as a designer thing, as a way of trying to be kind of cool, hoping it will get media attention. Martin Maloney did it with *Lost in Space*, but his ambition was to get to Gagosian. We put on a space that had no pretence of underground – or at most a fragile underground. The idea of artists and independence is a delicate balance. There is independence, but there are also huge compromises, which is fragile. Even if you stick a gallery in a ditch, word gets round, you might get a helicopter come in with a collector. It happens and artists hope it comes as well. This was not a reaction to capitalism, they were squat shows because we had a space and whatever happens, happens. It was done out of love.

BH: Is there anyone you would have liked to include but didn't?

DT: No. I think if I were to do a show now there would be others but then it would be a very different show. Charles Burchfield, D.H. Lawrence's paintings. Actually I think there are one or two shows I would like to put on. But if I did that I would also be very happy to be anonymous in terms of organising them.

BH: Now the curator's name is often the most dominant. Is the most important element of an artist-run space that it isn't about the person or people running it? I remember when Vilma Gold opened, it took me two years to realise it was Rachel Williams who I was at art school with who set it up.

DT: I think some are set up in order to promote themselves; inevitably you do promote yourself by proxy. But the people that went to Bart Wells were such a small community. No one knew I had put a

show on. There was no need to promote it. We had to ring up people and tell them to come along. There wasn't a strong philosophical theme, I didn't approach Luke and say I must do this. It was largely organic and you had to fit around that.

BH: Like every good group show you build it around the work.

DT: Also there was no attempt by me to have my name on it. I wasn't interested in being a curator.

Left page:
Hayley Tompkins
*No Title*
2003
13 x 6.5 cm

*Untitled*
2003
16.5 x 10 cm

*Untitled*
2003
16.5 x 10 cm

All watercolour on paper
Courtesy The Modern Institute
/Toby Webster Ltd., Glasgow

Tommy Støckel
*Half Man Half Sculpture*
2002
Digital c-print
85 x 60 cm

Ulli Knall
*Oh La La*
2002
Painted ceramic plaque
15 x 20 cm

# BART WELLS INSTITUTE

3 Silesia Buildings, London E8

PRESS RELEASE FOR *THE FRAGILE UNDERGROUND*

## THE FINAL EXHIBITION AT BART WELLS INSTITUTE

For the concluding show, Bart Wells Institute presents a community of resistance, holding on to the international language of abstraction. A revolutionary form once engaged in urban transformation now lovingly reinvested for self-improvement and quiet community renovation.

The artists here, adopting Modernist techniques, materials and its spirit of sociability offer a new community arts project. Inheriting ideas from their half remembered teachers in the fledgling Soviet Union and at the Bauhaus, they offer a re-evaluation of the avant-garde. Once believed to be a pivotal force for social change, this community instead seem more at ease transforming these principles into private ritual, embarking on a contented retreat into the periphery and surviving happily on the margins. Here a nostalgia of disappointment and disillusionment is replaced by a sense of joy and optimism. A homely and pleasurable radicalism, where a glimpse of utopia still prevails in their hearts and in their lives.

The community members here are:

### TOMMY STOCKEL

A man consumed by his passion for the Modernist architecture that surrounds him or maybe just a fan of Constructivist and Dada theatre. A man wishing to become his dreams.

### DARIA MARTIN

A revolutionary love film and balletic ode to Modernist pleasure, depicting wistfully impatient youths eager for utopia.

### ULLI KNALL

A radical mystic ceramist, celebrating the body beautiful and healthy living, promoting the transformation of both mind and spirit.

### EVA BERENDES

A militant activist for home improvement, giving urban modernism a touch of warmth inherited from the ethos of the hippy counter culture.

### FLORIAN BALZE

A builder and architect of softened modernism...

### SCOTT MYLES

Skilled pencil drawings of a polite anarchist.

### HAYLEY TOMKINS

A quiet demonstrator making intimate wall drawings and graffiti for quiet meditation.

Private View Friday 31st January 7-10pm, exhibition Saturday 1st February - Sunday 9th March 2003.

Curated by David Thorpe.

The directors of the Bart Wells Institute, Luke Gottelier and Francis Upritchard, would like to thank the following people, without whom the Institute would not have been possible; Sam Basu, Brian Griffiths, Jamie King, Harry Pye, Johnny Gunshenan, Leigh McCarthy, David Thorpe, Kate MacGarry, George Asciak, Mark Aerial Waller, Siraj Izhar, David Panos, Mat Humphrey, Sarah Jones, Jet, Olivia Lory Kay and Jess Search.

## "OH WHAT HAPPENED TO YOU? WHATEVER HAPPENED TO ME? WHAT BECAME OF THE PEOPLE WE USED TO BE?"

If you were to compare the Bart Wells gang to The Velvet Underground you could say Francis Upritchard was Lou Reed, Luke Gottelier was John Cale, Sam Basu was Sterling Morrison, Brian Griffiths was Doug Yule. And I was a cross between Nico, Andy Warhol and Mo Tucker. I was definitely the best one. I had the best ideas and was the most sexy and the most cool. It's soooo ironic that they are all doing so well now. I thought they'd all end up working in Burger King. Anyway, who knows what the future has in store for them?

Brian Griffiths was always very friendly. I think it was my sister Matty who first introduced us. When I first met him he was based in South London. He worked part-time helping special needs kids, and in his spare time he made spaceships out of cardboard boxes.

I met Luke Gottelier through the painter Stuart Cumberland. Stuart and I used to work together in the Tate bookshop. We both liked the paintings of Pablo Picasso and the films of Woody Allen but we used to disagree a lot. Stuart used to say things like "there's no such thing as video art" or that "women can either have an interesting personality or be attractive but they can't be both." Anyway, one day Stuart told me about Luke. He showed me a book we were selling in our shop called *New Neurotic Realism* which featured Luke's photos. At this time I made my own fanzine. It was called *Harry Pye's Frank Magazine*. I was looking for artists to interview and I decided to interview Luke as I liked his work.

Luke and I met at the Theatre Bar on Charing Cross Road. Luke arrived holding a big bunch of flowers which I later donated to the lady at the bar. It turned out we were both fans of the sculptor Bruce McLean. McLean had once said that being an artist was the best job you could have as it meant you had complete freedom. He also thought there was nothing more important than being silly. He said "the only reason to be an artist is so you can be stupid. So you can cut your nose off and stick it on your arse if you want to." At Bart Wells Institute there was a lot of silliness which I think was quite exciting and it contrasted well with the less interesting stupidness that was going on in most other spaces. Luke and I were also both long term fans of Andy Warhol and it turned out we had a few mutual friends too. Luke introduced me to Sam Basu (a charming chap who made Kung Fu videos) and Francis Upritchard (a Prince Charles fan from New Zealand who liked stuffing worms and painting Union Jacks).

I put Francis and Luke in some shows I was curating. The first one took place in France. It was called *It May Be Rubbish, But It's British Rubbish*. The second one was inspired by William Blake's proverb of Hell and it was called *Too Much or Not Enough?* and took place in Soho.

I had begun working and collaborating with friends such as Edward Ward, Adrian Shaw, Johnny de Veras, Gordon Beswick and Mat Humphrey. When I was invited by Luke and Francis to be in the Bart Wells shows I invited my friends along with me. I'm not sure how happy they were about this and maybe a few toes were trod on. Johnny and Mat weren't just artists they were also curators and they had lots of ideas for shows and projects. Mat actually moved in and lived and worked at Bart Wells. He and Johnny helped me enormously with putting up both walls and work. I'd like to take this opportunity to say "thank you" to them both. A lot of the Bart Wells Institute shows were good. Visitors were often scared to go up the stairs because they looked like they might collapse at any minute. Yet people came from miles away to see those shows, they walked through some of the most dodgy parts of East London to climb up rickety staircases covered in bird shit. But it was almost always worth it. I was impressed with a lot of what I saw. I was a young man with a lot to learn about life and people skills. I was also ill a lot of the time and therefore probably not always a joy to be with. But I still think Bruce McLean's words ring true and being an artist is great. Sam is converting a string factory in France into an arts centre by hand, Francis is part of the Venice Biennale and Brian's work is everywhere. But my time will come, just you wait and see.

— Harry Pye

Harry Pye
*Whatever Happened to the Bart Wells Gang*
2009
Acrylic on canvas
59 x 42 cm

LUKE: "EVER SINCE I WAS SIX ~~ELSE ALWAYS~~ I WANTED TO BE A DANCER. I LIKE DRESSING UP AND BEING ADMIRED." THEN ONE DAY I WAS TAKEN TO THE POMPIDOU CENTRE IN PARIS AND I DECIDED THAT BEFORE I WAS 32, I'D BE THE DIRECTOR OF A MUSEUM OR GALLERY.

BRIAN = "I FIRST MET LUKE AND DAVID THORPE IN HULL when we were students at Hull Polly. Luke had lovely hair and was very well developed for his age. He'd obviously read loads of books.

DAVID — What I liked about Luke's paintings was that they were never asking questions. They were bold and brash.

Francis — Luke and I met when he came to my show.

HARRY: "We all met at Francis & Jamie's flat. The mailing list we used came from The One In The Other ~~the~~ Gallery where Sam had just had a show.

Luke: "Sam's show was really good because it was unlike _ _ _ _ and he blah blah blah

LUKE: "BLAH BLAH BLAH, 3 STOREY BUILDING IN MARE STREET BLAH BLAH."

FRANCIS: "BLAH BLAH, LOTS OF PIGEON SHIT BLAH BLAH."

HARRY: "I GOT A LETTER FROM FRANCIS EXPLAINING THAT SHE'D BEEN IN A SERIOUS BIKE ACCIDENT BUT THAT SHE, JAMIE & LUKE HAD FOUND A SPACE. ~~I'D NEVER BEE~~ ALTHOUGH I WAS THE ONLY ONE WHO'D LIVED IN LONDON ALL MY LIFE I'D NEVER ACTUALLY BEEN TO HACKNEY

SAM: "THE FIRST TIME I SAW THE SPACE WAS IN _ _ _ MY FIRST THOUGHT WAS, BLAH BLAH BLAH

LUKE: ANOTHER THING ABOUT THE SPACE WAS THAT BLAH, BLAH

"Hi Harry Me and Luke found a really good space but I've been in an accident. — Francis"

BRIAN: In 2000 I curated a show at Vilma Gold called, "These Epic Islands" and Sam contributed this great

FRANCIS — I was keen to see what kind of show Sam would curate but only in my wildest dreams ~~said I~~ "Tombs of the Fantasy Un

SAM: All my life I've wanted to put on _ _ when Luke saw _ _ _ _

SAM